The
CATERPILLAR
That ROARED
Awakening the Lion Within

A Parable About the Journey Toward a More Meaningful Life

Joseph S. Sturniolo
Daniel Christopherson

NEW YORK

THE CATERPILLAR THAT ROARED:
Awakening the Lion Within

ISBN: 978-1-60037-343-5 Paperback

ISBN: 978-1-60037-342-8 Hardcover

Published by:

MORGAN · JAMES
THE ENTREPRENEURIAL PUBLISHER™

Morgan James Publishing, LLC
1225 Franklin Ave Ste 325
Garden City, NY 11530-1693
Toll Free 800-485-4943
www.MorganJamesPublishing.com

Habitat for Humanity®
Peninsula
Building Partner

Cover Wrap & Interior Design by:
Heather Kirk
www.GraphicsByHeather.com
Heather@GraphicsByHeather.com

Front Cover Graphics & Concept by:
Carol Wiley
www.CWileyDesign.com

Inside Illustrations by:
Holly Glass and Carol Wiley

NOTE: This book is a work of fiction (as should be obvious). Any resemblance to actual events or locales or persons, living or dead, is entirely coincidental, if not completely inconceivable.

FIRST EDITION

WHAT OUR READERS ARE SAYING

Through this modern-day parable, Joseph Sturniolo challenges us to take a fresh look at our lives. He urges us to move out of our comfortable chrysalis to soar as we follow our dormant passions and purposes. This is essential reading for anyone asking themselves, 'What's next?'"

~Dr. Peter Menconi

"Like the book, *Who Moved My Cheese*, this is a great read for those dreading the voice of an empty retirement. This book is a rare find that evokes the issues and passions we all face as we consider our retirement. The passions we need in the fulfillment of our lives, in leaving a legacy, can sometimes get lost in the maze of misguided priorities. This parable, with its underlying guide, is a must read, insightfully well-written!

"I heartily recommend this book for corporations and businesses facing the retirement enigma of their employees. It has broad-reaching potential for all of us who need and want to leave a legacy."

~George Diachok , Chairman of the Board
Geneos Wealth Management, Inc.

"*The Caterpillar That Roared* is an entertaining story that is inspirationally enlightening for those navigating mid-life transitions. It is told through the eyes of a wise sage, a butterfly named Antonio, with a parabolic vision of the true God-given meaning of life. I believe this book can be a catalyst for change for those who follow the rights of passage within this journey."

~*Dr. Tom Melton, Senior Pastor, Greenwood Community Church*
Greenwood Village, Colorado

"This delightful story about caterpillars and butterflies is really about the courage and commitment we all need to engage in personal transformation. The journey is difficult and those who are willing to overcome their complacency, doubts and fears will accomplish it."

~*Jack G. Nicholson, Principal, SageQuest Consulting*
and the 100Fold Project

IV

This book is dedicated to every person who finds the courage to awaken the long-caged lion within and, hearing its roar, does not shrink from it, but instead follows its command.

TABLE OF CONTENTS

VIII

FOREWORD

"The Caterpillar That Roared is a parable that utilizes the metaphor of a caterpillar in search of his God-given gift. He is on a quest. Each chapter reflects a unique step in the journey. At the end of each chapter the main character, Antonio, provides us a moral that defines the context of the path and obstacles he has faced and perhaps a lesson to be learned from it. The theme of this book reveals the baby boomers' quest, the desire for purpose, and the means to attain and fulfill that quest. It is about leaving your comfort zone and finding your unique purpose in life. It is about overcoming fears and obstacles along the way with determination and perseverance. This book is highly recommended reading for those who would like help finding and pursuing their true passion in life. Most adults engaged in continuing education are motivated by an underlying quest for a more fulfilling life; and the knowledge, skills, and attitudes gained by further study are usually essential for awakening, navigating and experiencing a new direction."

Dr. James R. Davis, Dean
University College
University of Denver

ACKNOWLEDGEMENTS

We wish to thank many people for their contributions to this book: our mentors and guides who received various parts of the manuscript as it took shape. These include Holly Glass, Jay Brenneman, Jack Nicholson, Pete Menconi, Tom Melton, George Diachok, Dan Sullivan, Beth Moran, Erin Gibbs, Margaret Morrison, Jim Davis and Anne Christopherson.

AUTHORS' NOTE

Butterflies are insects of the order Lepidoptera. From egg to larva (caterpillar) to cocoon to chrysalis to emergence as a fully-formed adult butterfly, the life cycle of most butterflies seldom exceeds eight to nine months.

If you are reading this book to learn about the true lives of butterflies, then read no further, for that is about as much scientifically correct information about these insects as you will find herein, this being a parable, after all.

For one thing, the butterflies in this book can talk.

And we all know that is not so.

At least not as far as science has been able to determine.

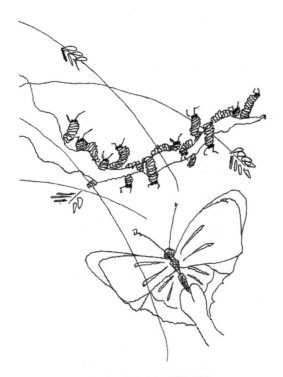

CHAPTER 1
Small Circle, Vicious Circle

The late afternoon brought with it a breeze, a puff of which caused Antonio's wings to flutter slightly, rousing him from his nap. He was groggy and a second, stronger puff nearly dislodged him from his perch atop the minister's rosebush.

The slant of the sun's rays now began to stretch the shadows, and the dark silhouette from the church steeple had cast its form over the rosebush and the adjoining hedge that rimmed the churchyard. Antonio shuddered slightly from the chill, and rued the coming of fall. Each passing summer grew shorter, it seemed.

He was in a nostalgic mood, musing that in his youth summertime had simply seemed less fleeting.

Drifting from the church was the sound of voices in song.

Time, like an ever-rolling stream, soon bears us all away;

We fly forgotten, as a dream

Dies at the opening of day...

Depressing but true, he thought. Then he yawned and turned slowly on his rose leaf perch to take in the vista of the hills encircling the vale and the village below. He loved this hour of the day in the valley, and how the trees stood in sharp definition, radiant in the amber light.

Below, in the village, wisps of smoke curled from the chimneys as hearths were stoked in preparation for cooking the evening meal. In the broad meadow that lay between the village and his hilltop vantage point, he saw a farmer and his dog rounding up a small flock of sheep. The dog ran nimbly around the sheep, making ever-tighter circles, then detoured, merrily bouncing around a recalcitrant ewe, and steering it back into the flock. Then the dog rested for a few seconds, panting happily and exulting. It was clear to Antonio that the dog was born for – and lived for – this task.

It was time for him to go about his responsibilities, too, he supposed. He yawned once more, then slowly stretched his wings. Although the wings' edges were a bit frayed, they were still handsome, painted in a magnificent pattern of black on a brilliant background of fiery orange and wine red. Moreover, they were still strong. Once the halting, and sometimes aching, first few beats of his wings lifted him airborne, they were able to carry him

2

farther, and with greater aerial acrobatic ability, than butterflies half his age.

With several beats, he rose up from the rosebush and rode the undulating breezes down into the meadow. As he did so, he mounted an updraft, then dipped and spun down again until he reached the limb of a young willow tree. The willow stood next to a brook that fed into a nearby river. The river separated the pasture from the village.

Along the willow's lower, yellow-green branches, a dozen bright green young caterpillars inched along, dining lustily on its spindly leaves and fattening themselves for the next phase of their lives.

One of the group took note of Antonio's arrival on a limb just below them and called to the others, "Hey, everybody! Look! Gramps's back."

That's what they called him, Gramps. Of course, Gramps was not their real grandfather, but they loved and venerated the old butterfly and thought of him as their Gramps, just the same.

They began to make their way down to where Antonio sat. He was pleased with their exuberance but grew impatient with their caterpillar pace, so he decided to fly up to meet them. There were only a couple of hours of daylight left, after all.

The old butterfly sat patiently at the junction of two branches, along both of which the caterpillars crawled as quickly as they could. Within a few minutes, they were clustered before him in a semi-circle, asking Antonio to tell them a story. Antonio's storytelling was famous throughout the meadow. He had a talent for combining his experiences and remarkable imagination into vivid descriptions of caterpillar and butterfly adventures. The

3

heroes of these tales often possessed unusual powers: caterpillars that could swim or spin cocoons of gold, butterflies that could lift heavy stones or fly to the moon.

Almost every tale concluded with a lesson of some sort. Antonio would always say, "And so, what do we learn from that?"

"Tell us a story, Gramps," said Melinda, one of the tiniest caterpillars in the bunch, but who was among the most assertive.

"And do you have a suggestion?" he said.

She thought for a moment. "I can't think."

He prodded her. "Go ahead. Start it. 'Once upon a time…'."

"Once upon a time," she said, stretching out the word "time," thinking, thinking.

"Yes?"

An idea came to her. She brightened and said, "Once upon a time there were no caterpillars and no butterflies living in this valley."

"Ahh," he said. "Now that is the start of an excellent story – and a true one!"

He began the story. "Once upon a time, and not so long ago, there were no caterpillars living in this valley. Not one. And, of course, there were no butterflies."

"So how did we get here, Gramps? How?" said Melinda. Several other caterpillars joined in the refrain. "Tell us how," they said. "How did we get here?"

"That story of 'how' is my story, too," he said. "It all started in the year 1634 – many, many miles from here, way beyond those hills, beyond the Atlantic, in a place called Tuscany, in a field of grapevines – a vineyard. I was born there and lived there, in a vineyard with thousands of other caterpillars. Life was good there. Until one day something happened that shook up our world..."

* * *

Antonio curled his long, bright green body around the uppermost stem of the grape plant. The plant was the last in the row, and the highest in the vineyard. From here, he could see rows and rows of vines, clinging to the undulating terrain. The grapevines, covered with morning dew, shimmered in the early morning sun; the hills that stood beyond the low stone walls that encircled the vineyard were dotted with poplars. On the horizon were rose-colored clouds. Such clouds often meant rain was on its way. It had not rained for 17 straight days. It was the second straight year of drought.

He surveyed the perimeter of the vineyard. As he did, he heard the rooster crow. He turned his eyes to the farmhouse and outbuildings that lay at the far corner of the property. The walls of the two-story house were made of stucco and were the color of clay. He watched as, one by one, the bright blue shutters were pushed open by the farmer's wife to let in the morning light.

Beyond the house and wall was the road to the village. Nothing more than a pair of wide ruts. Across the road and down toward the village was another farmhouse, ringed by tall, leafy trees. An olive orchard surrounded the back of the house, and beyond that was a peach orchard.

Antonio had heard tales of just how delicious the olives and peaches were; he longed to taste them. This was a silly dream, of course. He and his friends had idly speculated on how great it

5

would be to live in the peach orchard, but that, of course, would mean giving up their places in the vineyard.

That was almost unthinkable. There was a strict pecking order in the vineyard, and Antonio was among the "Higher-Ups," meaning he had always diligently followed the rules of the vine.

The rules were simple: each day do your best to climb higher on the vine, past hundreds of other caterpillars, climbing just as fast as you can – crawling over lesser caterpillars, pushing them off the stems as needed – until you reached the pinnacle of the vine, where the leaves and fruit tasted the sweetest – or at least seemed to. From there the Higher-Up ruled. No other caterpillar was to come, uninvited, within a foot of the Higher-Up's perch, his grape berries, grapes and grape leaves.

If challenged for his position, the Higher-Up might push grapes or grape berries down on their heads. Or if the Higher-Up's rivals were able to avoid the falling grapes, the Higher-Up would chew off a stem and use it as a weapon, to push the rivals from the vine.

It was either that, or the Higher-Up risked being pushed off himself. If the Higher-Up survived the fall, then he or she would be condemned to try to ascend the vine again, this time blocked by those whom the Higher-Up had stepped over before, who by now might have grown stronger, and whose bodies were not bruised from the fall.

The small, brownish vineyard moths that were always flitting above them seemed to enjoy this spectacle very much. The rise and fall, the struggles and backbiting. As caterpillars, they had, after all, endured the same rules and most failed in their efforts to get to the top. It was amusing now to view the folly of vine ascent from a distance.

Now, transformed from caterpillars into grape berry moths, they dropped their eggs on the ripening grape berries; within a few days, the eggs grew into larvae, otherwise known as caterpillars. Many of the moths would flit around the vines, exhorting their offspring to join in the race up the vine.

Antonio, a larger caterpillar, had maintained his position as the Higher-Up for several months. He was quick, crafty and ever-vigilant. Many would-be Higher-Ups had tumbled off the vine in trying to challenge him. It had been weeks since he had been seriously challenged.

Though he was the envy of those below, life at the top was not always such a great reward. True, the Higher-Up had the best views, and feasted on the plumpest, ripest grape berries as others below fought over what few grape berries were left. But he constantly could hear the whispers and giggles of those beneath him. Of course, they were jealous of his position. Who wouldn't be? Yet he also heard them deriding him for his appearance. While they were squatty, and dark green with purple rings around their heads, Antonio was much longer, a brighter green, and had no markings. "Il Brutto," they called him – the homely one. There were less than a half- dozen more caterpillars like him on the vine.

Often Antonio would feel lonely, and he would invite a few of those below to come visit him on his vine. They were suspicious of his motives, but they still would come, dine on the most primo berries, and indulge Antonio in his dreams of leaving the vineyard someday to sample the fruits and vegetables in the garden of the farmer who lived across the road. This was a wild dream, the caterpillars thought to themselves, but they indulged him as he speculated on how wonderful it might be there, with so many new things to sample. But of course they all derided him as crazy

7

when they descended back down the vine. No sane caterpillar would dream of leaving his Higher-Up position on the vine, or if he did, it would be to climb up a more promising vine. And no right-thinking caterpillar, whether a Higher-Up or not, would ever think of leaving the vineyard altogether.

One day, when Antonio had again invited guests to dine with him, among them was a bright green caterpillar who resembled Antonio in almost every way, although he was not quite as large. His name was Aldo, and his home-perch was just below Antonio's, a position with which he was quite content, having great respect and affection for Antonio and no wish to displace him at the top.

As he was in the habit of doing, Antonio once again idly mentioned his dream. "One day, I am getting off this vine, Aldo, and away from this dull life and find out what it's like in that garden." Of course, he knew in his heart that he likely would never do it, but he liked dreaming of it.

Aldo had heard this dream of Antonio's many times before; he had reflected on it himself many times. "You know, Antonio, I've been giving that idea a lot of thought myself.

"And you know what? I've decided it's a wonderful idea. This life is so very boring, so full of strife. And I'm sick of grape berries, grapes, and grape leaves and I would love to go see what olives and peaches taste like, wouldn't you? Of course you would! So why don't we go – right now?"

Antonio was taken aback. Was Aldo crazy? It's one thing to dream, but to actually do it, well, that was another thing.

As for the other guests, they all rolled their eyes and made their excuses, thanking their host as they departed down the vine, eager to get away.

Antonio and Aldo could hear them laughing derisively as they made their way back to their respective perches.

"Antonio, I'm serious. I'm going to go see what life is like in that vegetable garden – tomorrow. Are you coming with me?"

"Thank you for the invitation, but no, I am not," said Antonio.

"And why not?"

"Well, first of all, who knows what kind of trouble you could find there? There might be all kinds of hungry birds and spiders there."

"But we have those here, too."

"True. But maybe not so many as over there. And at least with the ones here, we know their habits, and that helps. There's a saying that goes, 'It is better to live with the devil you do know than the one you do not.'

"Besides, why would I, a Higher-Up, want to climb down from here and give up my position at the top of the vine? I worked hard to get here. I am not giving it up."

Aldo shrugged. "Suit yourself, then. I'm going first thing in the morning."

With that, Aldo said goodbye and descended down to his perch.

That night, Antonio got little sleep. He pondered Aldo's call to adventure. He wondered why he *really* had told Aldo no. Was he simply frightened of the possible perils of the journey and the destination? Or was he afraid to lose his position and, just as bad, be the object of ridicule? He had to admit that all of those concerns were on his mind, yet the pull of adventure away from his ordinary world was strong.

9

The next morning, Antonio arose from a brief and restless sleep. He curled himself around the tip of the highest point of the vine, stretched and took in the view from the valley. It was a gray morning and heavy, dark clouds peeked above the hills.

Down below he heard the stirring of the other caterpillars. They were cackling loudly and shouting to each other.

Antonio strained to hear what they were saying.

"Look at that fool! Leaving the vine, " called out one of them. "He doesn't know how good he has it."

"Where does he think he's going?" yelled another. "Does he think there's something better than here?"

"Or does he think he's too good for us?" yet another cried shrilly. She shouted down to Aldo, who now was several feet from the base of the vine and headed toward the road. "You idiot! Don't you have any sense? Stay within the vine!"

Aldo paused and glanced up at his detractors. He slowly shook his head then resumed his march.

Antonio's insides were churning. He had to admit he admired Aldo, even envied him. As for the catcalls the other caterpillars were launching at Aldo from the safety of their perches, he found the whole thing shameful. Who were they to criticize someone for having the courage to try something extraordinary?

And with that, Antonio called out to Aldo. "Aldo! Aldo! Wait for me!"

Aldo turned and looked up to the top of vine and waved his tail, beckoning Antonio to join him.

Antonio crawled down the vine, past dozens of startled, incredulous onlookers, many of them gasping, others clustering and whispering – stunned by this new development.

Antonio could hear the whispers and he knew full well why they were so amazed, and no doubt critical, of what he was doing. He was giving up his enviable position to embark on a dubious, potentially perilous journey. He himself once would have questioned the sanity of someone giving up such status on a whim. Yet here he was, descending from his lofty perch.

Minutes later, he reached the ground and sidled up to Aldo.

"Welcome," said Aldo.

"Glad to be here," said Antonio

"Looks like they are going to miss you," said Aldo sarcastically, gesturing toward the top of the vine.

Antonio looked up to his former perch. There already were several caterpillars tussling to claim the vacated perch as their own.

He shook his head. "I guess I must be crazy, giving up my position."

"That makes two of us. After all, I was just a foot below you on the vine. *Passare di mente*, forget them. C'mon. Let's get going."

The two began making their way toward the road as thunder rumbled in the distance.

Soon a brief, pounding rain began to fall, alleviating the drought conditions a bit but turning the vineyard field into a slick, muddy mess. Aldo and Antonio pressed on. It took them nearly an hour to reach the road separating them from the stone wall that enclosed the farm.

Antonio was exhausted. "Let's take a rest."

Aldo could not contain himself; he was focused on a long row of ripening tomatoes just inside the wall, eager to get his first taste. "Are you kidding? I'm hungry, my friend. For something different! I'm going."

"Suit yourself, Aldo. I'm going to catch my breath for a few minutes. I'll meet you there."

Aldo said, "Fine. I'll save some tomatoes for you."

Antonio curled himself into a semi-circle and watched as Aldo entered the muddy, rutted road. The going was slow as he weaved his way around the many deep puddles that had formed. He stopped near the middle of the road, panting.

Antonio smiled to himself, smug in the knowledge that he was not the only one who was exhausted from the hours-long journey. He also was pleased that the rain was letting up to just a few drops; he was now almost ready to resume the trek.

His contentment soon evaporated as he heard the noise of an approaching farm wagon drawn by a bony, aged black horse. At the reins was an old man covered in a black rain slicker; his fedora was pulled down nearly to his eyebrows. Wisps of white hair flared from underneath the hat, and his face was drawn and weary.

Antonio called out to Aldo to warn him of the approaching wagon, but Aldo at that moment already had taken note of the impending danger and was frozen with fear.

The clatter of the wagon wheels and the rhythmic clopping of the horse's hooves were growing alarmingly louder. Squeaks and groans came from the wagon springs as the wheels sank into the deep potholes.

Antonio surveyed the situation. The wagon was approaching, virtually in the center of the road, there being no other travelers in the way – except for Aldo. And Aldo was nearly dead-center.

He saw that Aldo at last was beginning to flee, headed to the far side of the road.

Antonio saw that Aldo was taking a risk, the possibility of being run over by one of the wagon wheels. If he would just stay in the middle of the road, the wagon would pass over him harmlessly.

"Stop, Aldo! Stay where you are!" Antonio screamed over the din. "Stay where you are!"

"What!?"

"Stay put! Or you'll put yourself right in the path of the wheels."

Aldo glanced at the wagon, which was now only a few yards away.

He did as Antonio had begged him. He stayed where he was, curling himself into a tight ball, tightly closing his eyes.

Meanwhile, hundreds of yards away in the vineyard, the other caterpillars had taken note of the impending crisis, those living in the vines closest to the road relaying the details to those farther away until, one-by-one, all the caterpillars were on the edge of their vines, watching the drama. They were transfixed.

Now the wagon was coming closer, separated from Aldo by perhaps just one or two more revolutions of its clattering wheels. Aldo opened his eyes briefly then closed them again. The ground was now trembling.

13

Up on the wagon, the old man's eyes widened a bit as he took note of a very large water-filled pothole. He yanked on the reins, shouting a command to the horse. The horse veered to the side of the road. That shifted one of the front wheels to a path leading directly toward Aldo.

Antonio saw what was happening and screamed, "Aldo! He's trying to avoid the pothole! Jump into the pothole!"

But the noise from the wagon was now too loud.

"What?! I can't hear you!"

Antonio shouted out the instructions again, but Aldo was no longer taking heed. He was scrambling to avoid the wheel, inching away as quickly as he could.

Too late. The wheel ran over him, embedding his remains in the mud.

Antonio gasped, then turned his head. He did not want to see.

The wagon rumbled by, curving back toward the center of the road.

In the vines there was a loud, jumbled chorus of comments reflecting on the horror they had just seen. There was grief expressed among some, but the loudest voices were those who previously had condemned the journey of Aldo and Antonio as foolhardy. What they had witnessed had confirmed their most deeply-held belief. Stay within the vines.

Antonio lay still for nearly an hour, stunned. *If only I had shut my mouth and not begged Aldo to stay in the center of the road. If only I had not suggested the idea of leaving the vineyard for the farmer's garden, this misadventure would never have even begun. Aldo would be alive right now.*

The rain had faded; the sun was now beginning to emerge, its brilliance mocking Antonio's dark, brooding mood.

His heart was heavy with grief. There was no thought of continuing the journey. Not now. Not ever.

It was nearly dusk by the time Antonio returned to the base of the vine he had previously abandoned. He made his way up the vine just a few inches, coming to rest on a crumbling, rotting branch nearly devoid of grape berries. From above him came a few expressions of sympathy, mixed with reproach.

He did not blame them for feeling as they did. He, too, blamed himself.

From now on, his life would be confined to the vine.

*   *   *

"That's so sad, Gramps. Did you ever climb to the top of the vine again?" asked Melinda.

Antonio replied, "Not for the longest time. I didn't have any desire to at first. And I was embarrassed. I preferred hiding out at the bottom of the vine. But then, one morning I awoke, it was a beautiful day, and I decided I wanted to have the best view of the valley again. So I pushed and bullied my way to the top again. The others really resented me by then. But I didn't give a darn. I was on top again, and I was content, if not exactly happy, with my ordinary life in my ordinary world."

He surveyed their disappointed young faces.

"And so what did we learn from that?" he asked them.

15

A short, stubby young caterpillar named Valerie took a guess. "To stay within the vines?"

"Well, yes, at first I thought that was the lesson, but it wasn't," he said. "The lesson I soon learned is this:

*L*esson

"We all live in too small a circle of comfort. *If we want our lives to be meaningful and passionate, we need to move outside of our comfortable and seemingly safe little worlds. Pursuing our dream always means leaving that little world. That means taking a risk."*

17

CHAPTER 2
Weighing Fears

Weeks had passed since the tragic misadventure with Aldo, yet Antonio remained depressed. He could not get Aldo off his mind, try as he might. He was atop the vine again, but the view from the top brought him little joy. In fact, the sight of the vegetable garden, peach orchard and olive trees across the road was all too clear a reminder of the ill-fated journey, and so he kept his back turned away from that scene almost all the time.

Occasionally, he would once again invite some of the other caterpillars up to dine and enjoy the view. But now most of them found excuses to stay away. Since the incident, a few of the cater-pillars had expressed their sympathy to him, but most spoke pri-vately of Antonio as if he was a bit crazy, and they blamed him for Aldo's demise. From time to time, Antonio would overhear these comments, and he would become even more dispirited.

While the others spent their days eating ravenously, Antonio could barely muster an appetite. At a time when he should have been fattening up for the long cocooning slumber, he was actual-ly losing weight. He was beginning to look withered.

So, too, was the vineyard. Since the heavy rainfall on the day of Aldo's death, it had scarcely rained at all. The vines were starved for moisture and a late spring frost had further impeded their growth. What little was left of the grape berries was being devoured by the caterpillars.

To make matters worse, the farmer, walking along the long rows of the vines, would daily pluck away some of the caterpillars, flinging them to the ground and then stomping them to death under his boots. This was a losing battle, of course, because there were thousands of caterpillars making their homes in the vines.

As did all the caterpillars, Antonio looked on these daily encounters with the farmer as a sad but unavoidable fact of life. Each knew that the odds were the farmer's grasp would never reach him or her. There simply were too many of them.

But the caterpillars would soon learn that the farmer had dis-covered a way to turn the odds in his favor.

One morning, as Antonio scanned the vineyard scene, he saw the farmer at the far end of the field, holding an unfamiliar imple-ment in his hands. It had a long round barrel, with a can mounted crosswise at one end, and a handle at the other end. The farmer would withdraw the handle from the tube, then press it in again. A foggy spray, aimed in the direction of the vine, would then issue from the opposite end of the device.

Antonio called down to several caterpillars who, until then, had been oblivious to the farmer's actions. A few were curious enough to cluster on the edge of the vine and observe him. Antonio asked them if they had ever seen the farmer employ such a device before. They all replied that they hadn't.

Antonio was not deterred. He continued his watch on the farmer's slow, rhythmic advance down the rows. Antonio thought it was curious that the farmer this time made no attempt to yank caterpillars from the vines. Instead, he just kept pumping, spraying and moving along.

Antonio assumed that the farmer was putting the caterpillars at risk in some way. He just did not know how. As far as he could tell, no caterpillars were suffering or panicking or falling from the vines. Yet the farmer's indifference to removing caterpillars from the vines led him to deduce that the spray would harm them somehow.

He felt compelled to sound a warning – but a warning of what? He had no proof to back up his suspicions. Further, he knew that most of the caterpillars, while envious of his physical prowess, and his Higher-Up position, now questioned the soundness of his thinking. Aldo's death was evidence enough to them of the folly of acting on one of Antonio's notions.

Antonio was filled with anxiety, replete with misgivings. He felt a powerful obligation to somehow induce the other caterpillars to remove themselves from potential harm. But he also knew that if they acted upon his warning and then subsequently found that his concern had proven groundless, he would fall even fur-

21

ther in their eyes. And, whether he would admit it to himself or not, what they thought of him did matter.

For nearly a half hour he debated with himself over what to do, as the farmer advanced ever nearer.

Finally, he decided it was better to be prudent, even if it eventually might lessen his standing on the vine. He began to descend the plant stalk, shouting warnings and urging the caterpillars to get down and away from the vine. At first, several of them decided to heed his warnings. But the jeers and catcalls aimed their way by the doubters quickly caused them to abandon their plans to evacuate with Antonio. Antonio was upset that his efforts to sound the alarm had produced so little effect. By the time he reached the base of the vine, he found he had only two followers, Giorgio and Gina.

Both of them knew Antonio well, and considered him to be a friend, having been invited by Antonio several times to visit him on his perch. Like Antonio, they were different from most of the other caterpillars – bright green.

Giorgio, despite being the largest caterpillar on the vine, had never really used his weight and length to his advantage. Others marveled at his lack of success; some thought him to lack courage or to be lazy. Many taunted him as dimwitted, and he had long ago begun to assume they were right. Although he could have bullied his way upward, he simply lacked the motivation to get to the top. It held no appeal. In fact, little about his life held any appeal. It was all boring. And when he was bored, he ate. And he ate all the time. Other than eating, he lacked any motivation at all.

Gina was his opposite – in body and soul. She was frail but feisty, brainy and quite cunning. Rarely was she intimidated by the size and aggressiveness of most other caterpillars. She masked any fears she had with a sharp tongue and heavy sarcasm.

She used her intelligence to overcome her lack of size. She managed to establish her perch halfway up the vine by charting a route to the perch that required crawling across leaves and twigs too weak to support other caterpillars.

She was a restless thinker, always questioning life's "givens." Most of the other caterpillars around her considered life to be a simple proposition: you are deposited as an egg on a vine, you grow into a larva, a voracious caterpillar, ascending as high up the vine as you can. Next, you spin a cocoon and it hardens into a chrysalis, protecting you while you sleep a long sleep, awaiting your metamorphosis; then you emerge, fly about for a short while, drop some eggs, and finally die. Gina believed there must be more to life, but felt fated to live her life as it was. She saw no way out, had no vision of where her life could lead her, and no one was there to show her the way.

Until now.

That's when Antonio had urged her and the others to follow him down the stalk and off the vine. She had fretted for a bit before following Antonio away from the vine. She was fearful of leaving but even more fearful of staying – not because of the fear of death but the fear of living in the way that all the others did.

* * *

Antonio paused in his narration, closing his eyes briefly, recalling the scene. One of the young caterpillars, named Andrew, grew restless. "And so?" he asked stirring Antonio from

23

his reverie, "Since hardly anyone was following you, did you think about climbing back up the vine?"

"No, I didn't," said Antonio. "For one thing, I would have been too embarrassed to turn around and go back. For another, I thought our lives might be in danger."

"So, were you able to convince any others to come down and join you?" asked Melinda.

"No, I quickly gave up trying. After all, most of them already thought I was out of my mind. And after what happened with Aldo, I thought maybe they were right."

"So what was the lesson learned," asked Andrew.

"The lesson Giorgio, Gina and I learned from those who did not join us in leaving the vine was that some things we really *ought* to fear are outweighed by the fear of change, the kind of fear that confines us in a cage of our own making. That blocks the journey we are meant to make.

"In other words:

Lesson

"Our circle of comfort is surrounded by a wall of fear. *There are few fears greater than leaving the place where we are comfortable, but there are few rewards more meaningful and purposeful."*

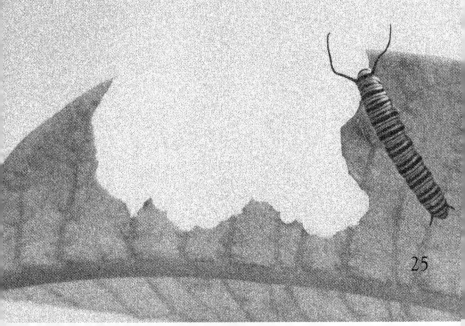

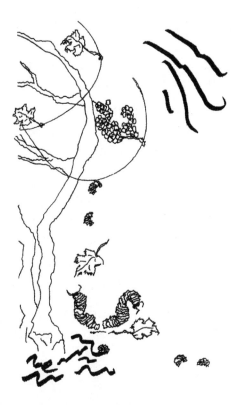

CHAPTER 3
Dying on the Vine

N ow the three of them – Antonio, Giorgio and Gina – stood at the foot of the vine, staring up at dozens of other caterpillars who had elected to stay behind. Some of them on the vine called down to them, derisively. Others urged the three of them to come to their senses and mount the vine.

"Remember what happened to Aldo," said one of them.

"*Always* stay within the vines," said another.

Antonio shrugged. Then he said to Gina and Giorgio, "So, I guess you two are the only ones foolish enough to follow me, right?"

Gina replied, "There might be others who agree, Antonio. And they'd not be foolish, either. Maybe some of them just haven't been able to make their way down the vine yet." She turned to Giorgio for support.

He looked up and down the vine and saw no one descending to join them. "She's probably right," he said. "I'm sure there'll be others. They're just slow, that's all."

Antonio took another long look at the vine. The taunts had slowed down. Maybe others *would* join them, after all.

Instead what he saw were caterpillars turning their backs on them; they had returned to scrounging for food on the withering plant.

"You *can't* just let them stay there," Gina said. "They're going to die."

"Maybe. Maybe not," Antonio said.

"What do you mean, 'maybe not'?" she said indignantly. "If you don't believe in it – in *yourself* – then why did you urge us all to follow you?"

Antonio sighed. "Fine. Here's why." Then he explained his reasoning – the strange new device in the farmer's hands, the spraying. And the farmer failing to resume plucking caterpillars off the vines.

He concluded, "I think he may have found a new way to do away with us."

Gina reflected for a few seconds, then said, "So, that makes sense. Doesn't that make sense to you, Giorgio?"

He nodded.

"Explain it to the others," she said to Antonio. "Just that way. They'll listen to you. You're the Higher-Up, after all. Go back up the vine! Quickly!"

"I *was* the Higher-Up," said Antonio. "But no more."

Gina summoned Giorgio to her side. "Arch your back, Giorgio" she commanded him.

"Huh?"

"Arch your back! Antonio needs a pedestal."

He looked at her quizzically. "A what?"

"Just do it!"

He arched his broad back and she scrambled up to its apex, then shouted up to those on the vine, "Attention! Attention! Please listen to what the Higher-Up has to say! Let him explain! You are in danger! "

A few curious caterpillars moved to the edge of the vine, looking down, evincing some interest. Then came a few more. And a few more after that. Now there were perhaps two dozen of them. Gina was heartened. She turned to beckon Antonio to the top of the pedestal formed by Giorgio's broad back, to further explain the reasons for his alarm.

But Antonio was not there.

He had departed, moving away as quickly from the vine as he possibly could.

She dropped to the ground and struggled to catch up to him, followed closely by Giorgio.

"Wait!" she called. "You can't leave them behind. They'll listen. If you just explain!"

But Antonio moved steadily into the shadow of a tall tree alongside the edge of the vineyard. The two others, catching up with him as he sat impassively at the base of the tree, watched them approach.

"You can't just turn your back on them!" Gina said. "They need you!"

"They won't listen to me. *You* tell them."

"They won't listen to me. *You* they will. You're the Higher-Up."

"Are you deaf? You want me to repeat it? I am not the Higher-Up anymore. It's not my problem," he said.

She glared at him, but he was unmoved.

Giorgio said gently, "Maybe just one more try?"

Antonio said, "I wish I were the great leader you think I am. But apparently I am nothing but a leader just of two – the two of you. If you believe my warning, then suit yourselves and follow me. As for the others, well, if they're right, they will have the last laugh."

With that, he inched across an exposed tree root, then followed it to the trunk and began climbing straight up.

Gina and Giorgio silently followed.

The three of them assembled near the tip of a slender tree branch. From there, they could watch the vineyard. They could see the farmer now had completed spraying the last vine in the final row. He paused, removed his broad-brimmed straw hat, then mopped his forehead with his sleeve. He turned and strode across the field in the direction of his house. He stopped at the first row

30

to inspect the vine. He shook some leaves and from them fell some caterpillars, lifeless.

Antonio, Gina and Giorgio gasped.

They recoiled as the farmer swept even more corpses from the vine. He smiled and nodded his head, appreciating the results of his work.

"It is just as you said it would be, Antonio," said Gina. "Exactly what you feared."

Antonio did not respond. He now trained his eyes on the vines closest to their vantage point on the tree. He could see caterpillars writhing, their bodies contorting. He could hear them moaning and wheezing. Some of them lost their grip on the vine and fell to the ground, breathing their last breaths.

Antonio slowly shook his head. Giorgio's eyes began to shed tears. Gina was trembling. She could no longer look. She turned away and curled herself into a tight ball.

The three of them could hear the farmer exulting to his wife as he entered the house. They shuddered.

"You saved our lives," said Giorgio. "You saved us."

Antonio turned toward him, his eyes blank. "If only they had respected me. If only I had been *worthy* of their respect. If only I could have made them listen. If only, if only..."

Giorgio said, "You did the best you could."

"You think so?" Antonio asked. He bit his lower lip and bobbed his head several times, pondering.

"Maybe you're right. Maybe that's the best I could have done. Then I guess I'm off the hook, right?"

As he said that, the leaves began to flutter wildly. Strong gusts of wind shook the limbs. In the distance, they could see a cloud of red dust billowing away from the desiccated vineyard. Everywhere, dead and dying caterpillars were blown off the vines, lifted by the wind, cascading to the ground, scuttling in small swirls.

*   *   *

"And the caterpillars on the vine, did they all die, Gramps?" asked Paul, whose eyes were misting.

"Most of them," Antonio replied.

"But it was not *your* fault," said Melinda. "They should have listened to you. After all, you were the Higher-Up."

"Getting to the top, well, that alone, does not make you a leader," he said.

"But you tried," Melinda said.

"Not hard enough. Not what I was called to do. Not in my position. I could have gone back, as Gina had urged me. I could have maybe persuaded a few of them – at least some of the ones on *my* vine – to escape. But I didn't want to risk being humiliated anymore than I already had been. I didn't want to risk being seen as a failure again."

"And what was the lesson you learned?" asked Melinda.

"The lesson I came to learn was this:

*L*esson

"**All of life's rewards come to those who are willing to break through the wall of fear, follow their heart and pursue their passions.** *You cannot achieve a higher purpose if you are too worried about failure or what people will say.*"

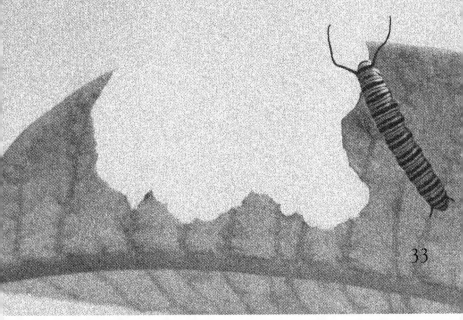

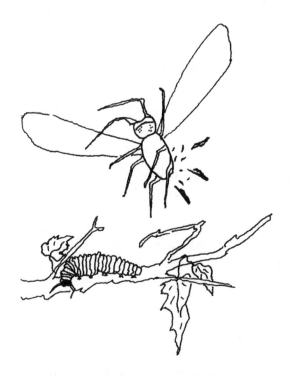

CHAPTER 4
An Unbidden Advisor

That day – at long last – on the heels of the wind came a brief, cleansing rain. By noon the sun shone brilliantly on the vineyard and all of the thirsty vines now stood more erect, their leaves and grape berries glistening.

Sweet, humid air hung above the vineyard and the meadows surrounding it. A gauzy haze hung above the farmer and his two young sons as they inspected the vines, chatting gaily as they plodded through each muddy row, speculating that perhaps now the drought was over.

Across the road, in the fruit orchards and vegetable gardens, a similar scene played out with another farmer and his wife. They strolled side-by-side, occasionally kneeling to inspect a budding plant or reaching up to cradle and admire a nascent peach, lemon or apricot.

The mood was markedly different in the tree where the three survivor caterpillars had taken refuge.

They had scarcely spoken since witnessing the demise of the others. Each of them had inched away to his or her branch. They had little hunger, but occasionally they would nibble at a tree leaf. They found the leaves to be bitter. Even Giorgio had little appetite for them.

Antonio gazed down on the vineyard; his head drooped over the edge of a branch. He took no consolation in having been right. Instead, he was saddened by his failure to convince so many to get out of harm's way. As to fulfilling the role of a Higher-Up, he judged his failure to be complete. Not only had his reckless dreaming led to the death of his friend Aldo, it had also killed his influence with those whom he was supposed to have led.

While he ruminated on this, he did not notice that Giorgio had sidled up behind him. As he began to back up from his precarious position on the branch, Antonio was startled to bump into him.

"Oh – sorry, Antonio."

"It's all right. But a little warning would have been nice."

As he spoke, Antonio noticed that Giorgio did not look well. His color had faded to a pale green and he appeared to have lost some of his formidable girth.

"Are you not feeling well?" Antonio inquired.

"I'm all right. Just feeling a little weak, is all. I can't say I much care for the food up here."

"I agree."

"Maybe – I was thinking – maybe it might be safe now to get out of the tree and go back to the vineyard."

"Might be."

"I mean, what do you think? That rain helped. The vines look a bit better now. And the grape berries, they've gotten plump again."

"Yes, they have. A little. Or maybe they just look better when you're stuck up here."

"Maybe. Anyway, I was thinking that we ought to give it a try."

"Suit yourself."

"I – we, actually – were talking about it. We wouldn't go without you."

Antonio bristled, "That's touching. But count me out."

A voice piped up from directly above them. "Apparently someone has lost his nerve." It was Gina.

Antonio and Giorgio tilted their heads and looked up at her. She was hanging by her tail from a twig a foot or so above them.

She let loose of the twig and plopped down onto the branch, right next to them. "I hope you don't mind my dropping in like this."

Antonio was not amused. "Very funny. Look, if you two want to go back to the vineyard, go. You can each have your own vine. Looks like each of you can be a Higher-Up now, since there's no competition anymore."

37

"I'm going to ignore your insult," she said. "Antonio, you know we can't stay up here much longer. We'll die of starvation. Look at Giorgio. He's gotten almost skinny."

Antonio replied, "Yes, I've noticed. And you're looking kind of sickly, too. But I don't trust it down there. I want to go somewhere else, but I have not the slightest idea where."

"Well, then what do you have to lose by coming with us back to the vineyard? Yes, we know that it was the spray that killed everyone. But now, with all that rain, how could there be any more spray left on the vines?"

Antonio sighed. He had no enthusiasm for returning to the vineyard. But on the other hand, assuming the farmer didn't return with the spray – and why would he, since almost all the caterpillars were dead? – and assuming the spray had been washed away, then returning to his ordinary existence on his cushy perch atop the newly revived vine was really the only acceptable alternative. He could not envision any other, try as he might.

"Fine. Fine. Fine. I'll go with you. Probably. Let me sleep on it, though. Now, if you don't mind, I'd like to be alone and do some thinking and maybe get some sleep."

His companions quickly complied with his request and headed off to the far side of the tree, arriving just as dusk fell. The sun settled behind the hill to the west, and a cooling breeze whisked into the valley. The result of the cooler temperature combining with the warm, humid ground was a low fog that rose a few feet above the vineyard and the adjacent meadow. Then, above the fog, hovered hundreds of fireflies.

Antonio watched the fireflies, their luminous abdomens winking in the gathering darkness. He wondered what the purpose was of their lights. *Wouldn't that just make them easier prey at night for ravens and other hungry birds?*

If he were a firefly, he thought, he would play it safe and never let his light shine.

He mused on that a while, finding the firefly display a welcome distraction. He realized his mood had lightened somewhat. He was beginning to feel at peace with the idea of returning to the vineyard. Not delighted, but almost content.

Soon he fell asleep. He slumbered for an hour or so until he was startled awake by a light tap on his back. Was it a vicious spider? A ravenous bird? He spun his head around to see what it was. He was surprised to see it was a firefly – dancing above him and casting a pulsating glow.

The firefly spoke. "Having sweet dreams, my friend?" It was a female voice, dulcet but strong.

"Wh-what?"

"I said, are you having sweet dreams?"

"No. Not that it's any of your business. I don't dream anymore. At least not daydreams. I try not to."

"Really?"

"Really. It doesn't pay."

"How sad."

"In fact, I've learned a dream can backfire and become a terrible nightmare."

"So, it's best not to have a dream?"

"Exactly."

39

"How so?"

He explained about acting on his dream of visiting the fruit and vegetable farm, that it had led to tragedy. That, in turn, caused the loss of confidence and respect among those who had once trusted in his judgment as the Higher-Up, ultimately resulting in their demise.

"So now what do you plan to do?"

"I plan to go back to my ordinary, everyday life. Back to my home in the vineyard. Tomorrow."

"Not such a good idea, Antonio. Trust me. The vineyard is poison. And not just the kind in the spray."

"Why is that? And just how do you know my name?"

"I know everything about you."

"Is that so?"

"It is so."

"And may I know your name, please?"

"My name is Angela."

"And why is going back to the vineyard such a bad idea, Angela?"

"Let me shed a little light on that for you," she said, her abdomen brightening. "First, the vineyard is not really your home."

"No?"

"Never has been. Not for you. Not for Giorgio. Not for Gina and for quite a few others, actually."

"How so?"

"It is a place where you have allowed yourselves to become comfortably parked. You and your friends and others of the same stripe found it comfortable in those surroundings. You and they found life came easily on the vine. You all could out-shine the grape berry moth caterpillars with no problem. You are stronger and smarter. Getting your fair share of the food was never a problem. And, for you, ascending to the position of Higher-Up was also no problem."

Antonio nodded slightly, in agreement.

"But of course once you attained your lofty position, the thrill was gone, wasn't it? And so you began dreaming about a new adventure, something more thrilling."

"That is true. I'll admit it. And look how it ended up."

"It ended up badly because you dreamt the wrong dream."

"How's that?"

"You set your sights too low, on the wrong thing. You thought by merely moving to your neighbor's farm you would find happiness there."

"Perhaps."

"No, definitely. But happiness is not given as a gift. Your gift *is* your happiness."

He tilted his head, perplexed. "What?"

"On the day we are conceived, each of us is given a gift, Antonio."

"So?"

41

"And when we discover what that gift is and employ it to a noble end, then true happiness ensues."

"Is that so?"

"Oh, you've most definitely been given a gift, Antonio. Most definitely."

"Apparently this gift has nothing to do with the requirements of life as a Higher-Up," he declared bitterly. "Otherwise the birds wouldn't be out there every day, feasting on the corpses of all those dead caterpillars lying in the vineyard."

"Your gift might or might not have been helpful to those who died. That is not for me to say."

"And so, you know so much about me, tell me, what is this gift I've been given?"

"No one can tell you what your gift is. They may possibly observe it. Many may think they know. They may tell you what they suppose it to be. But only *you* can actually apprehend what your gift is. You simply need to discover it or rediscover it, and just as important, discover who may benefit from it. And then it will become both your passion and your happiness. Believe me, you were born to do great things, Antonio."

"Right," he said sarcastically. "And so where do you propose I start? You say the vineyard is poison. Then perhaps I should lead Gina and Giorgio to another vineyard? Would I find my gift there?"

Angela's abdomen began to glow an icy pink. She was annoyed. "Are you not listening to me? Didn't I say you were born to do great things? Now you suggest that maybe you will go to another vineyard and make your home among some other grape berry caterpillars?!

"Is that what you want – to live your life among a pack of little caterpillars whose lives are as drab and dull as their coloring? Whose only adventure comes from dodging spiders and birds? Do you want to lead that kind of life again, then enter and later emerge from your cocoon, only to flutter around the vineyard for a few short, uninspired days, your only goal to deposit eggs on the grape leaves? Is that what you want?

"Have you not already determined that you and your friends are *not* like them? The vineyard – any vineyard – is not your home. Understand? You've never felt at home there, have you?"

"It was not so bad. I had it made."

"A life led without passion or purpose, without employing one's gift – and to use it to help others – is worse than bad. It is pointless, abysmal. It is the sin of sloth."

"So then why won't you tell me what my gift is, so I can put it to use…?"

"I told you already, you've got to find it for yourself."

"…or whom this so-called gift is supposed to benefit?"

"Like your gift, you must discover that on your own. And to do that, you must leave your comfortable, everyday, ordinary world, Antonio. Take a look inside your heart. Then take a risk. Seek out your gift, then share it. Ask your two friends to join you. And the sooner, the better."

Both were silent for a few moments. Then he spoke, his voice brightening.

"You know, I never did feel like I *belonged* with most of those caterpillars."

43

"Of course you didn't."

"And I'm not sure, but I *think* I see what you mean. Maybe."

She replied, "In the end, I know you will have found this lit-tle talk…illuminating. You see, Antonio, that's *my* gift."

And with that, she flew away into the night.

* * *

"And so, did you find your gift, Gramps? Did you?" Melinda asked Antonio.

"Not right away. But coming to know that there was a gift to be found – that was a gift, too, in a way."

Andrew said, "So that was the lesson you learned?"

"That was one of the lessons, yes. There was another more fundamental truth I came to understand that day. The lesson learned was this:

Lesson

"We must all make decisions about our passion and journey alone, but we will not get very far in that journey if we try to do it alone. *Everyone needs to form partnerships with others and most need mentors or teachers to help guide them along the way."*

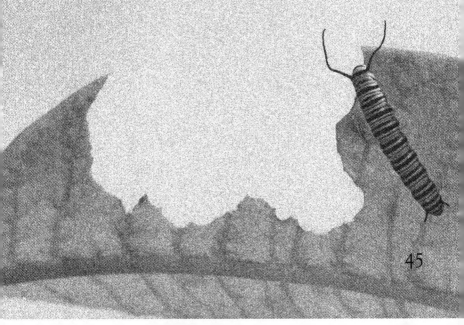

CHAPTER 5
Making the Leap

Antonio finally slept well that night, not arising until well after sunrise. He had had a pleasant dream. In the dream, he was no longer a caterpillar but a magnificent butterfly with a flying ability unmatched by his peers. He was not only adept at aerial acrobatics, he also had the ability to fly tirelessly for great distances, and with uncanny navigational powers. While other butterflies relied upon the direction and angle of the sun to set a course for home, Antonio could find his way home even when the sun was directly overhead or obscured by clouds. He could even navigate at night. It was as if he had an innate compass.

In the dream, his legendary skills had led a flock of geese to him to ask for help. They told him they had lost their way to their distant home, and implored him to lead them there. He agreed to do so and assumed the lead position at the apex of the flying V formed by his followers. He and his followers were flying high above the sea on a moonlit night and into the morning. The morning sun rose and cast Antonio's shadow down onto the still, mirror-like water. He looked down to see that the shadow's shape was not his but that of a griffin – the beast of myth with the head and wings of an eagle and the body of a lion. He swooped down to see his reflection. What he saw was that his head was no longer that of an eagle. It had now been transformed into the head of a lion, encircled by a heavy mane.

He turned to the geese and then roared mightily, calling to them to keep pace with him.

Though he was going somewhere he had never been before, he was absolutely certain of how to get there, and the geese followed him without question.

The dream ended abruptly, however. He was roused from his sleep by a tap on his head. Gina and Giorgio were sitting across from him with the sun at their backs. Another hot, dry day.

"Good morning. Ready to go back to the vineyard today?" Gina asked.

Antonio was not quite awake. "Huh?"

"You said yesterday you were ready to leave and return to the vineyard."

Antonio replied, "Ready to leave, yes. For the vineyard, no."

He then told them of his visit from the firefly and her advice. "She said, 'Happiness is *not* a gift. Your gift *is* your happiness,' and she said the gift is within me but to find it I needed to look elsewhere. Not in the vineyard."

Giorgio and Gina were perplexed.

"I don't get it. It sounds like a riddle," Giorgio said.

"Me neither," said Gina. "I don't get it."

"If this gift is in you already," she said, "why do you have to go somewhere else to find it?"

"She didn't really explain that but she said the vineyard is poison."

"So where are you going?" asked Giorgio.

"To the sea."

Gina and Giorgio were incredulous. They had heard of the sea but all they knew was that it was a place of seemingly endless water. No trees. No plants. No vines. No place for a butterfly to light.

Without waiting for their next question, Antonio related his dream. "I know it was just a dream. But something about it felt quite real. I just know that my gift has something to do with flying. And I know in my heart it somehow involves the sea, not this place. So that's where I am headed. And you are invited to come with me," said Antonio.

Gina and Giorgio looked at him as if he were daft.

"That might be all right for you, Antonio, and finding your gift and *your* happiness. Maybe *we* would like to find our gifts, too. And who's to say we cannot do it here?"

49

Antonio replied, "Angela says we weren't made to be in this place. Assuming we don't die of the poison, life is too easy here. Don't you see? This place demands little or nothing of us. No special gift is needed. Just the ability to crawl, to chew, and to endure the boredom."

Antonio saw the slow dawning of recognition in their faces. "Come with me."

"Just a minute," Gina said. Then she and Giorgio withdrew to a nearby branch of the tree to confer.

As they did, Antonio slowly pivoted his head, surveying the valley scene. At this hour, the sun washed over the landscape, bathing everything in its amber glow. Everything stood in sharp relief. Everything stood nearer. The suede-colored hills, the billowy trees and the teardrop shaped trees that formed undulating columns along the road and the vineyard rows. *This is a beautiful place*, he thought to himself. *Truly beautiful. I will miss it.*

He began to realize he was having second thoughts about leaving and quickly shook them off. *I must do this while I have the nerve, and while the dream moves me.*

In the distance, he noted a horse-drawn cart on the road, cresting the hill and headed in the direction of the vineyard. The wagon was apparently heavily loaded, and the horse moved slowly, even as the cart moved downhill.

Antonio began to hatch a plan.

As he did, Gina and Giorgio approached.

"Yes?" Antonio said.

Gina said, "We've decided to join you. But we might not go as far as the sea."

50

"Fine. Still, I'm glad to hear it."

She replied, "We don't quite grasp this idea of having a gift, but on the other hand we don't know if we can trust the safety of the vines anymore."

"Then follow me," Antonio said.

He led them out to the end of a very long tree limb, extending out over the road, about twenty feet above it.

"When the wagon is just below us, we jump in," Antonio said. "The road follows the stream. And the stream leads to the sea."

Gina balked, "Jump?! From way up here?!"

"Can't we go down to a lower limb?" pleaded Giorgio.

"If we take the time to go lower, we will miss out," Antonio said. "It's almost here."

"But there will be another one, sometime," Gina said.

"But we might not ever have the nerve again," countered Antonio.

They leaned out to watch the approaching cart. Antonio could see they were not quite far enough over the road to drop down straight into the cart. He gestured to a slim branch that arced out from the tip of the limb. "Hurry! Up the branch! We need another foot or so to make it.

"Now!" cried Antonio.

They scrambled as quickly as they could, and now all three of them were on a slender twig jutting out from a slender branch. The cart was not quite below them yet. Then the wind rustled the branch, nearly shaking them from the twig. Giorgio slipped, almost losing hold.

Then Antonio gave the command. "Jump!" With that, he plunged into the cart, landing atop a pile of grapes.

"Go! Now!" he yelled up to Gina and Giorgio.

Gina was trembling. Giorgio had now regained his footing. "Hold on to me," he instructed. "We'll jump together." Then he grabbed her and twisted around her, like a pretzel. "Here we go!" he said, as together they rolled off the tree and into the cart, unhurt.

The three of them clambered to the top of a small mountain of grapes inside the cart and watched the vineyard and the valley recede into the distance. All three reflected quietly. They knew there was no turning back.

*   *   *

Melinda asked Antonio, "And, so, Gramps, did the cart take them to the sea?"

"No, not directly. More like a sea of doubt," Antonio said.

"A sea of doubt?"

"One that can pull you away from your dream. Pull you away in its undertow."

Valerie said, "And the lesson learned was…?"

"As I said before, what encircles our comfort zone is a wall of fear. How do you break through that wall? That was the lesson I eventually learned:

Lesson

"The only way to break through that wall of fear is to grow confident in your passion, your purpose, for the rest of your life. *If you follow that passion, it's like a mariner in the middle of the ocean; he relies on having a compass that always — not just sometimes — points to true north. You can't get lost that way. If you believe in yourself and are clear about what you want to contribute to the world, then your compass needle stays pointed to true north."*

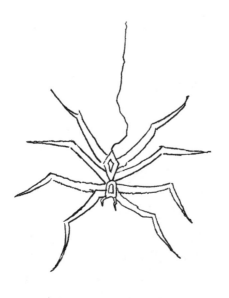

CHAPTER 6
The Obstacle Curse

After the first flush of adrenalin had passed, the three caterpillars sat atop the heap of grapes in the cart. They were sublimely pleased and proud that they had taken such a daring step toward seeking their dreams. The cart creaked and bounced along the crude road. The road's path hugged the stream leading to the village and the sea beyond. A new, exciting world opened up to them.

Soon they came to a monastery vineyard. Monks in brown robes paused from their labors to share a few pleasantries with the farmer who drove the cart. The farmer reached back into the cart to remove a cluster of grapes for the monks' inspection, causing Antonio, Gina and Giorgio to panic and briefly withdraw into the dark recesses of the grapes. They heard a lively exchange between one of the monks and the farmer, and slowly drew themselves out into the daylight again.

As the farmer drove on, the broad valley eventually narrowed between two towering hills. Both hills were festooned with terraces bearing vines and hilltop houses. The caterpillars had never seen such terraces before, or houses of such size and impressive bearing. Such wonders!

As they traveled, the threesome munched on the grapes and the grape leaves, a vast and seemingly endless banquet. Finally having eaten their fill, Gina and Giorgio began to doze off. Antonio, though, was still too entranced by the passing scenery and discoveries to sleep. Now, as the cart rounded a massive rocky abutment, Antonio's eyes widened as, down below, a breathtaking panorama of the village and the sea came into view. Antonio was euphoric. The prospect of seeking out his calling in this amazing place made the risk of leaving home for an unknown world all worth it.

He did not want his companions to miss what he was seeing, so he quickly awakened them from their nap. They, too, were jubilant about what they saw, Giorgio at first thinking he was still dreaming.

"No, it's not a dream," Antonio told him. "It's real!"

The three of them spent the next few minutes excitedly sharing their observations about what they were seeing, pointing out specific structures, including a walled castle that sat atop a hill overlooking the village. They speculated on what life was like in the scene that sprawled invitingly before their eyes, and what it might hold in store for them.

Gina and Giorgio thanked Antonio repeatedly for convincing them to leave the vineyard and accompany him on this quest for their dreams. Antonio basked in their praise, and while feigning humility, did not deny to himself that they indeed had a reason to be grateful.

The cart now swung around a gentle switchback as it descended further toward the village. As it did, the cart passed through an archway of trees that blocked the view of the village. The three travelers were disappointed to lose the vista, but pleased for the temporary break from the hot sun that the trees' shade provided.

Their euphoric mood was suddenly shattered by the cacophonous calls of a pair of ravens perched on a tree limb above them. The startled caterpillars looked up to see the birds launching themselves from the tree, and then swooping toward the cart. In quick succession, they alighted on the back wall of the cart bin. The caterpillars knew that it was them, not the grapes, the ravens were after.

For the second time on the journey, they found themselves burrowing furiously into the grape pile, trying to put themselves out of the way of the darting beaks of the ravens. Giorgio, though, was slower to react than the others. One of the ravens had managed to grasp him at the tip of his tail and was yanking him repeatedly. Giorgio was fighting for his life, curling himself around a grape stem. Thus tethered, and with his extraordinary strength, he was at last able to free himself from the bird.

Antonio and Gina called to him, asking if he was safe.

57

"For now, yes," he yelled back. "But I don't think they are going to give up."

Giorgio was right. Through the filtered light above him, he was able to glimpse the birds, pecking at the grapes, raising the clusters and tossing them aside.

The three caterpillars, seeking to escape, moved deeper into the mass of grapes. As they did, the grapes became more tightly bunched. Progress slowed to a halt. Antonio became separated from the others, sandwiched between a mass of grapes and the front wall of the cart bin.

He could hear the ravens moving the grape bunches about. The farmer was singing gaily, oblivious to what was happening right behind him.

From somewhere on the far side of the cart, Gina shouted, "Antonio! Giorgio! Please help. They are coming so close! Do something!"

Antonio called out, "I'm coming!" Giorgio echoed the cry. But Antonio realized he needed a plan.

Using grapes as his ladder, he scaled to a point just below the top of the grape pile. Cautiously, he poked his head out and saw the birds still tearing away at the pile, tossing bunches of grapes over the sides of the cart.

And still the farmer sang merrily, paying no heed to the activities behind him.

Antonio waited for the opportune time and reached across to gain a hold on the back of the farmers' seat. He thrust himself toward the seatback, and then climbed onto the nape of the farmer's neck. The farmer reached back quickly to swat what he thought must have been a fly or a bee. As he did so, Antonio released his grasp on the farmer and leapt back into the bin. This caught the eye of one of the ravens, who hopped over rapidly but in vain as Antonio burrowed out of sight.

The farmer, wondering what had been on his neck, swung around and spied the two birds, one of whom was caught with a small bunch of grapes in his beak. The man cursed at them, removed his hat and swatted in their direction. Cawing and screeching, they flew away, retreating to a safe perch in a tree nearby.

They continued to caw menacingly as the farmer passed below them. He shouted another oath at them as he replaced the hat on his head.

An hour or so later, the three caterpillars reconvened at the top of the grape heap, keeping a vigilant eye on the sky. Though none of them expressed it aloud, each separately thought that making the break from the vineyard was perhaps not to prove as idyllic as they had thought. Antonio felt it most deeply, recalling how his first venture outside the ordinary world had resulted in Aldo's demise.

Their mood soon brightened, however, as the cart finally reached the bottom of the hill. In front of them lay the outskirts of the village. Eager not to miss a thing, they strained for better vantage points atop the heap of grapes, unobstructed by the farmer's back.

Minutes later, they were taken aback when the farmer turned the cart to the right, away from the village, and mounted a narrow road leading up to the castle they had seen earlier.

When, at last, they reached the castle, they could see that it was not really a castle at all, but instead a fading old hillside villa,

59

surrounded by a low, crumbling wall. At the entry, atop two rusted iron gates, was an archway bearing two words forged in wrought iron: "Villa Bacchus."

The cart passed through the rusted gates and encircled the villa, from which no sign of human activity emanated. Weeds grew in the yard that fronted the villa; still more sprouted from the cracks between the cobblestone drive.

As the cart rounded to the back of the house, the farmer was greeted by a cheerless, sunken-faced young man. They gathered, by his few terse comments to the farmer, that his name was Vincenzo and that he was annoyed because they were late. The farmer apologized.

Vincenzo directed the farmer to back the cart into a nearby barn built of stone blocks. He then positioned a dozen crates near the rear of the cart. The farmer released the tailgate on the cart and the two men, with wooden rakes in hand, began transferring the grapes into the crates.

As they did so, Antonio, Gina and Giorgio tried to scramble together toward the front of the cart. None of them liked what they saw – a dark, cobweb-infested, sickly-sweet smelling room filled with grapes. Their hope was to remain with the cart and be transported to the village, or at least to the crossroads where they could jump off the cart and make their way into the village on their own.

That hope was dashed, however, as the farmer, with one motion, swept them and the grapes into a crate. Vincenzo and the farmer lugged the crate to a corner of the barn, placing it atop a shoulder-high stack of other crates bulging with grapes.

The trio had tumbled apart during their unceremonious dumping into the container. They called to each other and finally rendezvoused atop the crate. They watched as the farmer's cart departed in the late afternoon sunlight and Vincenzo closed the doors.

Now, only a few shards of light filtered through the cracks under the doors and through one small window laced with cobwebs. Slowly, their eyes adjusted to the dimness. They began to survey their situation. How depressing! The place reeked of grapes fermenting, and the huge cobwebs visible in the rafters and the corners of the window signaled the threat of big spider trouble. Antonio wondered to himself how many caterpillars had become their dinner.

Nonetheless, he did his best to cast their situation in a positive way. "Perhaps, this will not be so bad a place to spend the night," Antonio told his worried looking companions. "It is not as if we are trapped in here. There is more than enough room under the doors to allow us to get out. We can make our way to the village tomorrow.

"And who knows?" he said brightly, trying to cloak his own doubts. "We might just find what we're looking for right here."

"Here?" Gina and Giorgio said in unison.

"I don't believe it!" said Gina.

After that outburst, they were surprised to hear a voice calling to them from within the crate directly behind them.

"Don't jump to conclusions," came the voice. "I, myself, have found everything my heart desires right here within the pleasant confines of this abode."

It was a plump grape berry caterpillar, just like one of the thousands with whom they had lived back in the vineyard. His head was all that was visible; his trunk was immersed within the ruptured wall of an overripe grape.

61

He continued, in a slightly tipsy voice. "Here all is provided for...sustenance for the body in copious amounts, and plentiful grapes that have done a magnificent job of transforming themselves into an amusing wine...all without the help of human hands. Or without the help of human feet, for that matter," he said with a chuckle and a wink, punctuating the latter observation with a loud hiccup.

A titter of caterpillar laughter sprung from various locations within the mountain of crates, informing Antonio, Gina and Giorgio that they had plenty of company within the barn.

Gina engaged the drunken caterpillar in a conversation, hoping to gain some clues about their situation. He told them that he had been in the barn for two or three days – he couldn't really remember which. In that time, he had witnessed dozens of crates being removed, some of them with caterpillars inside...most of them "a bit tipsy," he said, and thus not terribly concerned about what awaited them outside the barn.

"There was one – a spunky young lass, who was dumped in with the grapes in the stomping bin, but she managed to escape and found her way back here. She said we all are destined to be crushed underfoot along with the grapes unless we get out of here. Hah! What a pessimist. She tried to slink out under the door later that day but, as she did so, she was exposed by the daylight, and – just like that! – she was set upon by one of the biggest, most ugly spiders you'd ever imagine.

"It's a crying shame," the fellow continued. "As for me, I've made my peace with my fate. Better to become a part of the wine than become one with the spider." And with that, he cackled and submerged himself back into the vinous grape.

Antonio and his friends shuddered, and then scanned the barn for spiders. They could see several crawling along two mammoth webs crisscrossing the upper corner of each door. They spotted two more lowering themselves on silky web threads toward a crate located at the far side of the barn.

"Our best chance is to wait until after dark," Antonio said. "We need to get out of here when the spiders are not as likely to spot us. In the meantime, we had better burrow deeply into this bunch of grapes, so as not to be in plain view."

Later, it became clear that the moon was not going to abet them in their plans to safely exit under cover of darkness. It was large and full, shining through the barn window and illuminating a host of spiders busying themselves with their webs, and dining on the insects trapped within them, all night long.

Antonio said, "We will just have to wait until Vincenzo takes this crate outside. Then we will have to jump out before we reach the press."

Gina and Giorgio concurred.

"Let's have something to eat, and get a good night's rest," he continued. "Tomorrow we will need our strength and our wits about us.

"And, Giorgio, be careful that the grapes you eat haven't begun to ferment. Better yet, stick to eating grape leaves tonight, will you?"

Giorgio agreed. However, the next morning, he and Antonio discovered it was Gina who should have been cautioned about the grapes. She had somehow managed to consume a fermenting grape and had become drunk. They found her passed out, hanging precariously over the top edge of the crate. They looked up in time to spot a huge, ugly spider ascending a vertical support of the crate, headed her way.

"Get up, Gina!" Giorgio cried. At the rate the spider was climbing, it was clear that both he and Antonio were too far away to grab her in time before the spider got her first. They continued screaming at her, stirring other caterpillars in the barn to join them in exhorting her to rouse herself and escape the spider's clutches.

The spider had just placed a leg on Gina's back when she awoke; she turned, groggily, face-to-face with the menacing insect. She was hung over! Her head was pounding mightily. Her stomach was convulsing. And she was paralyzed with fear.

"Do something, Gina!" Antonio yelled. "Quickly!"

And an instant later, she did. She vomited into the face of the spider, spewing a hot, slimy projectile of undigested grape rinds, leaves and alcohol-laced grape juice.

The stunned spider abruptly stepped back a few inches, allowing Gina to slip into the mass of grapes. The spider made a desultory effort to locate her, then departed.

It took a few minutes before their hearts stopped pounding. Then the three of them began calling to each other, finally gathering near a top corner of the crate.

Antonio and Giorgio both nuzzled her affectionately, and then rebuked her for failing to avoid the fermenting grapes.

"I hadn't intended to imbibe, but it started to feel pretty good once I started," she said. "And I had plenty of company, I can tell you that," she said.

"Yes, we could hear the reveling and the drinking songs all night long," said Antonio. "Didn't dream you would be a part of it. It nearly got you killed."

As he said that, the doors of the barn slid open and Vincenzo and a portly woman wearing a white, wine-stained apron entered the barn. They began removing some of the crates. As the crates passed by them, Antonio and his companions could see that at least half of the crates contained wine-addled, groggy caterpillars, almost certainly headed for their demise in the press.

Then the woman grabbed their crate and made her way outside. Squinting in the sunlight they could see Vincenzo heaping the grapes, caterpillars and all, into the press, and two young women beginning to remove their shoes.

As they had previously planned, the three caterpillars jumped to the ground from the upper corner of the crate. They landed relatively painlessly in the soft, red dust. Then they began crawling back toward the entry gates and the road toward the village.

The way to the village was much longer than they had supposed. The crawl was arduous, made more so by an unseasonably hot day.

An hour into their trip, they had put scarcely a hundred yards distance between themselves and the entry gates. Giorgio and Gina had been lagging behind Antonio most of the way, and when he made a comment intended to encourage them, he heard no response. He turned to see the two of them in the middle of the road, motionless and panting.

Antonio backtracked to join them.

"We'll never make it," Gina told him. "Not today, anyway. Not in this sun."

65

Giorgio, breathing heavily, muttered his agreement.

Antonio did not know what to say to spur them on. He could see that they were suffering, as was he.

Then they heard behind them the sounds of a rapidly approaching donkey cart. Walking alongside the donkey was a boy, maybe 12 years of age.

With great effort, they managed to extricate themselves from the path of the grape-laden cart, which was obviously headed for the storehouse at the Villa Bacchus. As they lay in the sparse grass at the edge of the road, Antonio watched the wheels effortlessly rolling by. As he did so, an inspiration came to him, a way to both ease and speed the journey down the hill and to the village.

Placing his head against the tip of his tail, he formed his body into a wheel. Gina and Giorgio looked on as he tried and failed to thrust himself down the road. He had some difficulty, at first, maintaining his momentum and steering in the direction he wanted to go. Gina and Giorgio laughed at him, but then he challenged them to try it themselves. Less than ten minutes later they, too, were rolling down the road, occasionally falling over, laughing at themselves, and resuming their cart-wheeling.

Finally, they reached the bottom of the hill and the crossroads, where they turned and took the road leading them into town. There was no downhill grade anymore, and thus no gravity to assist them in cart-wheeling, but they found that by thrusting forward at the top of each rotation, they could maintain their forward momentum, albeit slowly and with considerable effort.

Once they entered the village, they crawled along at a moderate pace, happily marveling at each newfound discovery. For their safety in avoiding horses, carts and pedestrians, they stayed out of the mainstream of traffic, clinging to the edge of the cobblestone and dirt streets.

Since they had departed the villa not long after dawn, it was still relatively early in the morning when they arrived at the central piazza and the open air market. The caterpillars were energized by the vitality of the market, the animated verbal interchange between vendors and patrons, and the wonderful smells.

To one side of the marketplace a small crowd was gathered around a wagon bearing a steel cage. Curious, the three caterpillars made their way to a viewpoint safe from being trampled by some person's boot. What they saw inside the cage was a lion. He had a huge but matted mane; his body was old and withered, every bone in his ribcage was visible. There were signs of mange on his fur. He paced back and forth within the cage.

The caretaker explained to the onlookers that the animal had been kept in the private menagerie of a contessa. She had recently replaced the old lion with a young cub and no longer wanted the expenses of feeding the older one. So, he explained, the old lion had been sold off and was being transported to join the menagerie of a once-powerful family in Naples whose fading fortunes meant they could no longer afford to commission the capture and transport of a young lion fresh off the boat from the African continent.

The lion paused for a few seconds, staring implacably at the crowd. Then, without provocation, he roared – startling the crowd. Then he roared some more, the noise echoing across the piazza.

"Sounds fearsome, doesn't he?" said the caretaker. "But you know, only yesterday, while we were camped in the country, I had just fed him and hadn't realized that I had failed to completely secure the cage gate. I turned away for a moment and then looked back. He had nudged the gate open. He was staring right at me, trying to decide if he should jump out of there and run. And you know what, he just watched me as I closed and locked that gate. Never tried to escape. Amazing, huh?"

The lion roared again, this time even louder.

"Guess he's sorry he missed his chance," the man said, chuckling.

Then the crowd began to thin, turning back toward the market.

Realizing how hungry they were, the caterpillars set off to plunder a food vendor. In their search, they passed an old man with a long, gray drooping moustache. Before him was a small table draped in red felt. Propped up on the felt were several small displays. One was covered in earrings and amulets; inside each was a small wildflower. Another board displayed at least a dozen paper-weights, and in almost all of them they saw, entombed within the glass, a variety of butterflies and large moths with distinctive markings, their lifeless but magnificently colored, outstretched wings frozen in time.

The three of them were aghast, and they wondered aloud if a similar fate might befall them. Giorgio suggested they turn back and head home to the ordinary world of the vineyard.

"Suit yourself," said Antonio. "I can't blame you. It appears that life here has risks I never imagined. It wouldn't be the first time I underestimated such dangers."

"No, I guess it wouldn't," Gina replied caustically. "Looks like we have traded in one set of risks for another, probably worse."

"So, are you thinking of returning, too?" asked Antonio.

"Perhaps. But not until I've had something to eat."

68

She then turned and headed toward the food vendor's stall. Giorgio and Antonio trailed along behind her. Antonio had a heavy heart and no real appetite, but he followed his companions as they crawled up a leg of the vendor's table and into a neatly stacked carton of tomatoes. They slipped under the top tier of tomatoes and clustered on one very large, ripe tomato. They each had gnawed deep into this new treat before a small human hand began rolling away the top layer of tomatoes and removed theirs.

"Look!" exclaimed the girl, who could not have been more than five or six years old. "Look at that!" she said to her brother, displaying the tomato and the three caterpillars.

He was a bit older than she but not too old to marvel at the sight of the caterpillars, all three of them frozen with fear. "They're beautiful! But we had better find another tomato for Mama. This one now has holes in it."

One of the vendors, a wizened old woman with a shrewish face, clad all in black, took note of the caterpillars. "Caterpillars! Give me that tomato and I'll put those creatures where they belong – under my foot!"

The little girl was alarmed. "Please don't hurt them. Please? Let me take them home?"

Her brother chimed in, "May we? We'll pay for the tomato."

The woman relented. "Just take it. No one would buy it now, anyway."

The children made off with their prize.

Soon, the caterpillars found themselves inside a lush, flower-filled courtyard behind the children's home. Gently, the children placed each one of them on a lemon tree and watched

69

them as they crawled about the lemons and feasted on the leaves. Things were looking up as far the caterpillars were concerned. This was paradise.

Later, the children placed the caterpillars inside an empty box, with holes punched into its lid, and then transported the box into the house. They placed the box on the tiled floor of the kitchen, removed the caterpillars from the box and attempted to engage them in a foot race. The caterpillars were mystified as to the children's intentions, but they knew they would not harm them.

Hearing the children loudly exhorting the caterpillars to race, their mother entered the kitchen to see what the commotion was about. She scolded the children. Not only was she unhappy to have the caterpillars inside the house, she was upset that instead of fulfilling her request for a perfect, ripe, unblemished tomato, the children had brought home a tomato pockmarked with shallow yet quite visible caterpillar holes.

She shooed them out of the house and instructed them to keep the caterpillars outside. And she ordered them to go back to the market to buy a proper tomato.

The children placed the box on top of a narrow ledge adjoining the stairway to the courtyard, then left for the market.

Inside the box, the caterpillars grew restive. Except for the light shining through a few air holes, the box was dark. With Antonio standing atop Giorgio, and Gina atop Antonio, they tried to push open the lid of the box, but to no avail.

"So, this must be what prison is like," sighed Antonio. "I apologize to both of you. This was a stupid, stupid idea, leaving the ordinary world."

"Apparently so," Gina said with a huff. She retreated to a corner of the box without another word, curled up, closed her eyes and tried to sleep.

Giorgio just shrugged and likewise curled up in a corner.

Antonio slumped to the floor of the box, deeply depressed and angry with himself, but overcome with an anxiety that seemed to have nothing to do with being imprisoned in the dark. It was an overwhelming urge to be alone – to be accountable to no one, without the company of Gina or Giorgio or anyone else, for that matter.

An hour or so passed as Antonio waited for the children. He mulled his fate and that of his two friends. *Surely, they will return and open this box and free us. They've had their fun. Where are they?*

As he contemplated this, he and his companions were stirred by a sudden rocking motion. They assumed the children were back. Antonio remarked that, no doubt, soon the children would return, open the box and release them.

But it was the family's housecat who was rocking the box. Curious about its contents, she had crept down the ledge and was tentatively poking at the box. She did so several times, until it tumbled to the slate walkway at the base of the stairs.

The three terrified caterpillars spilled out onto the walkway and found themselves eye-to-eye with the cat. The cat crouched closer, inspecting them closely, then with her paw took a swipe at Giorgio, who skidded a few inches away, tightly curled into a trembling ball.

Gina, attempting to flee, wound herself into a wheel, rocked back and forth and finally began rotating down the gently sloping walkway and into the courtyard. For a moment, the cat just watched her, transfixed, then began to crouch, ready to spring.

Antonio saw that the cat would pounce on Gina if he did not do something very quickly. So, without the cat's knowledge, he clutched the tip of her tail. Antonio held on tightly as she flicked her tail twice. He then scaled higher up to the top of her tail. Annoyed, the cat turned her head and realized he was out of reach. Vainly, she began to spin.

Out the corner of his eye, Antonio could see Gina rolling farther away, past the center of the courtyard, with Giorgio rolling along not far behind her.

The cat once again began chasing her tail, hissing. Then, abruptly, she paused, hearing the back door open.

The children had returned. They laughed when they saw Antonio astride the cat's tail. The little girl grabbed the cat by the nape of her neck, hoisting her up so that her brother could remove Antonio.

He placed Antonio back in the box, leaving the box on the ground, with the lid open. The two children then searched all over the courtyard for Gina and Giorgio, but they were nowhere to be found.

When the children returned to the box, they discovered Antonio also had escaped. His heart still pounding wildly, Antonio had climbed a tree near the center of the courtyard as rapidly as he could, finally coming to rest on a slender branch at least ten feet above the ground.

After he caught his breath, he began calling to his friends. There was no reply. He waited a few minutes and tried again. Still no reply. He realized then he was alone. And he was surprised that he was not sad about that. For once, he felt accountable to no one and was relieved to be rid of the responsibility he felt toward his friends. It was a good feeling.

* * *

"Gramps, you saved Gina and Giorgio from that cat – and then you didn't want anything to do with them?" said Melinda.

"Well, it wasn't quite like that," Antonio replied. "I just needed some time to myself to figure out what I am – to find my place in the world, what my life was meant to become."

"Huh? You mean you didn't know who you were?"

"My life seemed to have been drawn up for me by others, by what others said, what they valued, the way things were done on the vine – the things that were accepted as important, like striving to be the Higher-Up. When I left the vine, I figured it was time I draw my own picture of who I was. Or what I wanted to become.

"Let me ask you, Melinda – do you have a picture in your head of what you want your life to be, where you want to go, what you want to do, and for whom, once you have your wings?"

She thought briefly. "Uhh…I guess I don't know. Not for sure. Just a random bunch of ideas. Kinda sketchy."

"Ahh – sketchy! Exactly. And that was the lesson I learned:

73

Lesson

"All works of art begin with a sketch. Life's next adventure is like an empty canvas. You don't necessarily know what the next brush stroke is going to be but you will recognize the final picture when you see it. Like every work of art, you must begin with a sketch. Sketches are the experiments that help you solidify the final vision for your life."

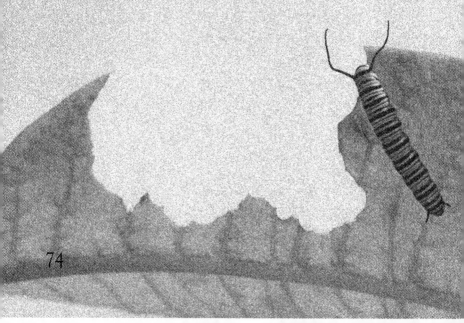

CHAPTER 7
Paint the Picture

Several days later, Antonio's life had taken an even more solitary turn. The strange feeling he had experienced while captive in the box had quickly evolved into an urgent compulsion. The result was that he had spun a cocoon for himself. The silky cocoon had hardened into a chrysalis and now was suspended in sweet, quiet, undisturbed darkness.

The transforming state of chrysalis, however, was not a suitably rapid one, and altogether too confining. He became bored almost from the beginning, and tried to make time pass more quickly by distracting himself in a variety of ways. To amuse himself, he summoned images and events of the past. Pleasant memories always seemed to be quickly swallowed by unpleasant ones, including thoughts of Aldo and his demise, and his own subsequent loss of face among his fellow inhabitants of the vine.

One day, an event happened that would cause him to put his time in the shrouded sanctuary of the cocoon to much better use. In a dream, Angela the firefly appeared.

"Angela! Is that you?"

"Yes," she said. "It is I. The question is, who are *you?*"

"You know who I am."

"Yes, I do. But do *you* know who you are?"

"I'm Antonio, of course."

"And who *is* Antonio?"

"I'm a caterpillar. Or maybe a moth. Something in between?"

"That's the body you are talking about. Your physical form. Is that what you are – merely a body that eats, sleeps and spins a cocoon?"

"No."

"And so what *are* you?"

"Inside?"

"Inside. What moves you? Delights you? What gifts have you been given? With whom – and how – will you share them?"

"While I'm inside this shell, that's what I hope to find out."

"Good. But if that is the case, why do you occupy yourself with thoughts and concerns of the past and whether you succeeded in meeting the expectations of others?"

"I don't know. To make time pass."

Angela then spoke at length about the opportunity he was being given, and thus far squandering, during his period of sanctuary. She encouraged him not just to rest or to ruminate on the past, but to shed the disillusionment the journey so far had brought. "Instead of being in such a rush, slow down, shut out the ordinary world, and use this time in the darkness to better *see*. You cannot move forward on your journey until you understand where you are, who you are and envision where you are meant to be."

"But I tried to envision that before. No picture ever comes to mind. Ever."

"You must begin to see the light *now*, Antonio, before you are thrust back into the world. Begin to paint the picture of what your life could be."

"Paint the picture?"

"In your mind and in your heart," she said. "Relax. Breathe. Recall your youthful dreams and the things you have done in the past that have most delighted you, just for the doing and the good that is done. Envision your future doing those things. Paint it in your mind."

And with that, her body pulsed, glowing brightly several times. Then she was gone.

Antonio awoke and reflected on what she had said. And so he began a more contemplative internal journey, shutting out all thoughts of ordinary life and calling to mind the things he had done so far in his life that had made him the happiest, the most fulfilled. Slowly, a picture was emerging – a painting of his purpose. It was fuzzy in places, with many lines and shadings still to take shape. But it *was* taking shape.

Thinking back to the moments that had produced the most joy, he realized that the common thread had little to do with having reached the honored perch atop the vine. It was, instead, the climbing of the vine itself – challenging himself to go farther than any others, pushing himself to do so rapidly, taking in new vistas the higher he rose. The other caterpillars had marveled at his strength and incredible endurance. They praised him for that, and he had to admit that he enjoyed the praise, but he would have pushed himself to the top in the absence of anyone else to witness it. It simply gave him great satisfaction.

His endurance and love of the climb he realized were coupled with an uncanny sense of direction that others on the vine seemed to lack. He was often amused by watching other caterpillars trying to find their way back to their starting points on the vine. They were frequently befuddled, backtracking and zigzagging, muttering oaths. He, on the other hand, could find his way around quickly, even on the darkest nights.

He recalled the time when he was still very, very young. During a restless sleep he had tumbled from the leaf on which he had been sleeping onto a leaf-top very far down the vine, bumping into grapes and leaves and slumbering caterpillars all the way down. Thus awakened, he was undaunted by the pitch-black darkness. Something inside him helped guide him unerringly through scores of vines right back to where he had started.

78

His willingness to explore, to push himself beyond the normal limits of others, and his innate compass – all these together, he realized now, comprised a special gift. But he also knew that it could be a gift of dubious value; his penchant for exploration had already resulted in disastrous misadventures for himself as well as those drawn to follow him.

Another week passed and then the big moment finally arrived. Squirming and thrusting, chewing through his crusty shell, he shucked his chrysalis and emerged, tumbling several feet onto a tree limb. He paused and squinted in the blinding daylight.

When his eyes finally adjusted, he scanned the scene in the garden. He had nearly forgotten how beautiful the surroundings were. Flowers of all kinds, budding fruit trees and magnificent rosebushes produced a kaleidoscope of colors and shapes. The lilting air carried with it a variety of perfumes. Truly the world looked more beautiful to him than he could ever recall.

As he looked around, he became aware of the presence of several butterflies flitting about a cluster of daisies, pausing occasionally to rest and slowly stretch their wings, basking in the sun. The colors displayed were a vivid reddish orange, etched with a remarkably-formed black filigree. *They are beautiful to look at,* thought Antonio. *And, oh, how they must be able to fly, as broad as those wings are.*

He twisted his head, hoping to compare his wings to the robust and gorgeously painted wings in front of him. But he was unable to turn his head far enough around to see.

Then he heard a familiar voice calling to him. "Antonio! It's us!" came the cry. It was Gina! Within seconds he felt a slight puff of air overhead as Gina and Giorgio hovered above him momentarily.

"Hi, Antonio," said Giorgio. "So what do you think of these?" He spread his wings, showing off their size and coloring.

Antonio was stunned. Giorgio was not a moth! Instead he was one of the butterflies Antonio had just been admiring.

"And how about these?" said Gina, also displaying her similarly impressive wings.

Antonio was speechless. She was spectacularly beautiful.

"And you look fantastic yourself," said Gina.

"I do?"

"Come on. Follow us!" she said. She and Giorgio then flew over to the birdbath in the center of the garden, settling along the rim.

To his delight, Antonio found himself fluttering several feet above Gina and Giorgio.

"Now what?" he called down to them.

"Follow us," Gina said.

She and Giorgio then flew a complete circle around the garden and settled upon the rim of a birdbath.

Giorgio was peering into his reflection in the water, transfixed by what he saw.

"He likes what he sees," Gina said to Antonio with a smile. "Why don't you look for yourself?"

Antonio tentatively crept to the rim's edge and looked down into the water. His eyes widened as he realized he was not a common, drab grape-berry moth as he had always assumed he would be. He was a magnificent butterfly.

"I – I'm a butterfly?" he asked.

"Nothing less." said Gina.

He peered into the water again. As he did, a brief gust of wind rippled the water, distorting his reflection for a few seconds. He was startled to see the head of a lion looking back at him. And it appeared to rear its head and roar. Then the water settled and once again he saw the butterfly he had become.

"I'm a butterfly!" he cried, turning again to view his reflection as he spread his wings, marveling at their beauty and size. He wondered why he had always assumed he was destined to be a run-of-the-mill moth.

Giorgio sidled next to him. "You show-off," he said to Antonio. "Your wings are as broad as a bird's."

Antonio could not disagree with him. His wingspan was indeed quite wide.

Then other butterflies from throughout the garden, curious to see their own reflections, flew from surrounding bushes and flowers, each finding a place along the rim of the birdbath.

Antonio couldn't help but compare himself to the others. All of them had the same reddish-orange color as he, but none had wings as large as his.

Realizing he was in possession of a special gift, Antonio decided to see how well he could put this gift to use. With two quick flaps of his wings, he lifted himself into the air and began a solo trip around the garden.

He first tried to see how fast he could fly. He soon was surprised at the results, as were the other butterflies down below, who let out "oohs" and "ahhs." He swooped down to a pink rose, challenging a hovering bee there to a race across the courtyard.

The result wasn't even close. Antonio won by a wide margin. His friends on the birdbath cheered.

Then he decided to see how high he could fly, and as he rapidly rose skyward, he was amazed to see the garden and the house below him quickly recede in size.

The view was spectacular. Ahead of him he could see nearly all the rooftops in the village and, beyond that, the sailboats on the sea, tacking into the breeze. To his right, he could look across and see the flowered hillside and the road leading to the Villa Bacchus. To his left was a broad, green, undulating plain checkered by a number of small farms.

Looking straight down to his right, he saw a slightly stooped elderly man walking slowly along the cobblestone street that flanked the garden. The man stopped and leaned on the low wall that separated the garden and the side of the house from the street. He tilted a pole of some kind against the wall and peered into the garden. Antonio sensed danger. Then he saw the two children – the ones who had once taken him and his friends prisoners – come walking down the street from the opposite direction. They stopped and greeted the man. Then all three of them entered through the gate into the garden.

Anxious for a closer view, Antonio descended almost halfway to the ground.

What he saw next was alarming. The man unfurled a net from the top of his pole and began slowly stalking a group of butterflies basking atop a hedge alongside the house.

Antonio dropped still lower for a better view. Now he could see the man quite clearly. He moved with a halting gait. Tufts of gray hair sprouted from under his straw hat. A bushy gray moustache hid his upper lip. This was the man from the vendor stall! The one with all the glass-entombed butterflies.

The man began swooping at the butterflies with the net. The children cheered him on, calling him "*Nonno.*" Grandpa.

After several failed swoops of the net, it was clear that Grandpa had caught at least one or more butterflies. The little boy ran into the house and very quickly returned with a clear jar with a broad cork lid.

Antonio descended once again, this time settling onto a tree branch right above the scene, but high enough to be out of harm's way. He watched as Grandpa carefully removed two butterflies by pinching their wings delicately between two knuckles, placed them in the jar, and replaced the lid, imprisoning them.

Antonio could see the butterflies fluttering madly about inside the jar, batting their wings against the side.

The little boy begged Grandpa for an opportunity to use the net, but he was refused. "Let me gather a few more first, Mario. Then your turn. Then Maria's."

He continued, "These are similar to painted lady butterflies." He held up the jar to inspect them. "In Latin, *vannessa cadui.* But the markings are different. See these big markings? They sort of look like a lion rampant, like something from a coat of arms. Very nice specimens. My customers will love these."

With that, he placed the jar on a ledge at the base of the steps leading up into the house. "Now I shall get a few more."

Followed by his grandson and granddaughter, Grandpa stealthily moved toward a far corner of the garden where several unsuspecting butterflies were napping on a brightly flowered bush.

83

The jar was left unprotected and Antonio flew over to the jar to inspect it, and perhaps give some encouragement to those trapped inside. Settling next to the jar, he could see that both butterflies, their backs to him, were almost motionless. He was alarmed, wondering if they were dying or merely just resting.

He crept around to the other side of the jar, hoping to communicate with them.

It was Gina and Giorgio.

He was stunned. Speechless.

Giorgio brightened at seeing his friend and batted his wings, rising an inch or two above the bottom of the jar. Gina weakly waved one wing.

Antonio could hear their muffled cries. "Help us! Please!"

But what could he do?

* * *

All in the semi-circle of young caterpillars surrounding Antonio were leaning forward, eager to learn the fate of the imprisoned butterflies.

Valerie said, "And so?"

Antonio said, "And so there was another lesson I learned."

She protested, "No. No. Not what the lesson learned was. What happened next?"

"Soon, soon. But first, the lesson I came to learn, which was this:

Lesson

"Once you are on the other side of your wall of fear that does not mean that the going will be easy. Quite the contrary. Many individuals will try to convince you to go back and many will try to slow you down and many will simply convince you that your purpose is not worthy of you. You will also face obstacles such as self-doubt, feeling unsafe and insecure, or being worried about how you will survive. Only the strength of your values and purpose will keep you moving beyond them."

CHAPTER 8
The Confrontation

Antonio stared helplessly into the jar. Inside, Gina was slumped over onto her side, her exposed wing shuddering briefly, stiffly, slowly collapsing.

By her side, Giorgio leaned over, looked into her eyes and said something to her that Antonio, his nose pressed to the jar, could not hear.

Giorgio looked up and shouted at Antonio. "She's injured. Banged into the side. Please, do something!"

Antonio shrugged, "I would if I could, Giorgio."

"You must!"

"But, I , uh, I…"

"Watch out!" screamed Giorgio, hopping slightly. "Behind you!"

In the reflection from the jar, Antonio saw Grandpa and the children returning toward them. Grandpa had the butterfly net, one hand clasped midway around the netting. Inside the netting was another butterfly, trembling.

"Grandpa! Look there! A big one!" said the little girl, pointing toward Antonio. "Come quick!"

"Oh, my! That's a beauty! And so large!" He picked up his pace.

Antonio lit out for the safety of a high limb on the tree.

"Look at that, will you?" said Grandpa. "He has wings the size of a young dove."

"Hope he will come back," said the girl.

"Let's be ready in case he does," Grandpa said.

Antonio watched as Grandpa reached into the net and pinched together both wings of the frightened butterfly. He carefully removed the top of the jar and dropped the third butterfly into it, careful not to let the other two escape. Then Grandpa resumed his hunt, promising once more to let the children have a try later.

Antonio stared anxiously at the jar and its prisoners. Grandpa returned and deposited two more butterflies in the jar. Antonio brooded about the fate of his two friends. *They're going to die in there.*

I know it. My fault. Again. Thanks to my stupidity. They trusted me. They followed me to this nightmare world. Why couldn't I have been content to stay where I was? Why?!

His dark thoughts were interrupted by the laughter of the children as they helped their grandfather corral several more butterflies.

What can I possibly do?

A female voice emanated from behind him, coming from the darkest, most shaded recesses of the tree, near the trunk.

"You won't know what you possibly can do until you do it," she said.

"Angela?" He turned to look for her, but she was not immediately visible.

"Over here," she said. He looked about and finally found her, poised atop a small twig bearing one tiny leaf. "You were expecting a glow? In the middle of the day? You're going to have to settle for enlightenment instead of light."

"Please, Angela. You see what's going on down there. You've got to help. Thanks to me, my friends are about to die. And so will the others."

He looked over his shoulder, downward. Another butterfly was being deposited in the jar. Now the boy took the butterfly net from Grandpa and began stalking a cluster of butterflies basking on a bush.

"Tell me, what am I to do, Angela?" Antonio implored. "Help me. What can I do? What?!"

"Do what you were born to do. Employ your gift."

89

"What? My flying? How could that help?"

"Employ your gift. We are only here for the briefest time. And that time is a gift in itself."

With that, she flitted off, out of sight.

Perplexed, Antonio sighed and slowly spun around to see what was happening with the butterfly roundup.

From below, he heard the little girl. "That's one for you, Mario. Now, my turn!" She snatched the net away from her brother and began a lively pursuit of a frightened butterfly. It twisted and dove. It was able to elude the girl, and then fluttered over the wall and into the street. Antonio admired its acrobatics. *That butterfly, too, has a gift somewhat similar to my own. Not nearly as good as mine, but enough to save himself.*

"I got one! I got one!" shouted the girl, running up to her grandfather who once again removed the lid and deposited the butterfly in it.

Then Antonio saw Grandpa reach into his pocket and remove a small, amber-colored bottle with a cork on the top of it. He reached into his pocket again and produced a small wad of unwoven cotton. He removed the cork and then turned the bottle over. Then he began tapping its fluid contents into the cotton.

An alarm bell rang within Antonio's head. He thought back to the farmer in the vineyard and his deadly spray can. The caterpillars gasping, dying and tumbling from the vines.

Then inside his head he heard Angela's voice again: *Do what you were born to do. Employ your gift.*

And then he swooped below, headed straight toward the old man.

*   *   *

The caterpillars were transfixed. But they knew by his pausing that Antonio would go no further in his account of this adventure until he had imparted the lesson.

So Melinda said, "The lesson learned?"

He said, "The lesson learned was this:

Lesson

"You will always face challenges that will make you doubt the wisdom of your intentions and your reasons for the journey. It takes courage to move forward when you are not sure what you will face."

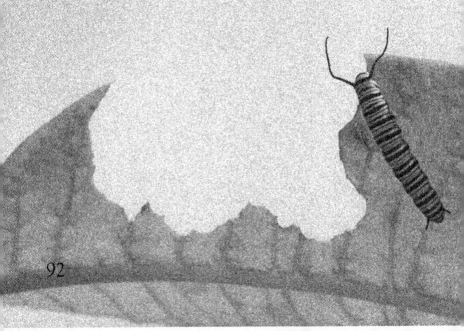

CHAPTER 9
The Battle

Oblivious to the fast-approaching Antonio above him, the old man was about to demonstrate to his grandchildren the next step in collecting butterflies.

"Now, children, before they do any more harm to their precious wings, you see what I am about to do here? This little rag will put them at rest, permanently."

Swooping right in front of the old man's nose, Antonio was still afraid but nonetheless very determined.

The old man was startled. He swung his head around quickly, unsure of what the blur had been that had passed in front of him.

The children were excited. "It's that big one, Grandpa!" cried the boy. "Can I get him?"

"No," said Grandpa. "I can't afford *not* to catch him. He's too valuable. He will make a very, very fine paperweight."

Grandpa quickly placed the soaked cotton on the ledge, next to the jar. "You stay away from that rag," he cautioned the children. "I'll put it in the jar once that big one's in there, too, with the rest of them."

He took the net from the girl and stalked off after Antonio, who was flying about the garden, shouting at every butterfly he could find to take refuge in the tree and stay there. Many had been napping. Some had just arrived. Others had assumed they were far enough away to be safe.

All of them, though, did not hesitate to follow Antonio's command. His self-assured presence matched his prodigious flying skills. Within a minute or so, dozens of butterflies flew to the tree. They sat and watched the spectacle below.

Antonio made another pass at the old man, narrowly escaping the swipe of the net. Then Antonio led the man on a meandering chase across the garden, back in the direction of the captive butterflies. He stayed just far enough ahead of Grandpa to avoid the net. Twice he stopped to let the old man – panting and cursing – catch up with him. Then Antonio would rise directly above the man, taunting him, challenging him to catch him. Each time, his strong wings and acrobatic skills managed to make the man miss.

By the time Antonio and Grandpa had arrived near the ledge where the jar sat, the old man was weary and very frustrated. He leaned for a few seconds on the ledge, catching his breath, with his eyes trained on Antonio, who hovered just in front of him, mocking him.

The man stood up again, muttered an oath, gripped the pole of the butterfly net firmly and took a quick stride in Antonio's direction. Antonio quickly darted to the man's left and began circling him. The man began spinning around after him, in vain pursuit.

Antonio's plan was to make the old man dizzy, then back him into the jar, hoping he would bump it off the ledge, freeing the butterflies.

Then he heard the faint voice of Giorgio, shouting from within the jar. "Get him Antonio! Get him!"

Antonio paused, stopping in mid-flight, hovering to turn and look at Giorgio, who was fluttering with excitement. A chorus of similar encouragement was coming from both within the jar and from the spectators atop the tree.

Distracted, Antonio inadvertently allowed the net to swoosh down upon him, enveloping him. He was trapped.

"Aha!" Grandpa exulted. "You're mine!"

And as he said that, dizziness overwhelmed him and he staggered backwards, knocking the jar off the ledge. It shattered on the stones, freeing the butterflies.

Grandpa turned and saw the seven stunned butterflies scrambling along the ground, trying to get their bearings.

95

"They're going to get away Grandpa! All of them!" shouted the boy.

"Get them! Get them!" yelled the girl.

The butterflies now had grouped together. Then they began to rise as one. Giorgio clutched the injured Gina, carrying her with him.

"Give me the net, Grandpa! Now!" said the boy. He did not wait for the old man's answer, grabbing the net away from him, with Antonio still trapped inside.

The boy was intent on recapturing all seven butterflies in one giant, arcing swoop. He raised the net quickly, snapping it high above his head. But the movement turned the net inside out, freeing Antonio, who flew down to the dazed but newly-freed butterflies and led them away to safety.

"Now see what you've done, stupid *bambino*," yelled Grandpa. "Give me that net! Now! Stupid! That one large specimen would have fetched more money than all the others put together."

The man seized the net from the child, but by then it was too late. Antonio had led the seven escapees to the top of the tree, where dozens of others received them with an enthusiastic welcome.

* * *

"Hooray!" the little caterpillars exclaimed.

"I guess you taught that old man a lesson, didn't you Grandpa?"

"I learned a lesson, too. The lesson learned was this:

Lesson

"In your journey, there is always at least one obstacle that may appear too large to surmount. **Courage to act and move through and beyond a daunting obstacle always comes from having a heartfelt purpose.** Knowing that your personal 'true north' always involves helping others takes you beyond thinking of only yourself and instead impels you toward making your contribution. Only when your journey centers on helping others will you feel the power and thus be moved by the passion of your journey."

CHAPTER 10
The Prize

Only a few minutes after the escape from the jar, the excitement among his butterfly companions already had begun to fade. One by one, the butterflies began departing the tree, flitting about the garden.

Except for Gina and Giorgio, who were on the far side of the tree, Antonio was alone. He was savoring his victory and enjoying the tranquility.

Down below, Antonio could see the little girl come out of the house with a jar of water for her grandfather. The boy fanned the old man, who was still breathing hard from his encounter with the huge butterfly.

Antonio had benign feelings toward the children. Even though the children had joined their grandfather in chasing butterflies, they also had rescued him and his two friends from the vegetable vendor. He and his friends owed these unlikely allies a debt.

His musing was interrupted by someone calling his name, not far behind him. Through the dappled daylight that shone through the leaves, he saw it was Angela. She was sitting on a twig, enveloped in a shadow only a yard or so away. Although it was dark enough for a glow to be visible, there was no light emanating from within her.

"You must have done well with your contemplations in that cocoon, Antonio," she said in a voice that was barely above a whisper.

"Angela!" He was happy to see her but alarmed by her wan appearance. "Angela, are you all right?"

She ignored his question. "You found it, didn't you?"

"Huh?"

"Your gift. Who you are. What moves you."

He paused and reflected on what she had said for a few seconds. "Why, yes," he replied. "That's true. I owe you for that."

"Not so much as you think."

"No, it's true," he protested. "I almost wasted all that valuable time in the cocoon. If it weren't for you, I would have been content back then to avoid all the trouble and enjoy my new wings for myself only. That's not what I was meant to do. That's not my destiny."

"And that destiny is…?"

"I feel a pull, Angela. To a place I've never seen before. Except in a dream. I can't really explain it. It came to me while in the chrysalis. I know there is a place where I – *we*," he said, motioning to a passing cluster of Painted Lady butterflies. "…where we and future generations are intended to be. It's that way," he said, gesturing to the north. "And it's very far away."

She nodded. "Knowing the way, and staying the course, that's all one ever needs to know, Antonio."

He nodded in agreement.

"Now, I must go," she said. "While you still have many days and many miles to go on your journey, I've done what I was meant to do, for you and for others, and I'm glad of it. I have a voyage of my own to make, Antonio."

And with that she teetered for a second or two, collapsed onto a leaf just below her, then curled slightly. She gave off one final, bright glow before gasping her last breath.

Antonio quickly moved toward her, but as he did a puff of wind blew her body off the leaf before he could reach her. He watched it swirl on an eddy of air, then miraculously rise far above the ground, a faint speck, dissolving into the sunlight.

He sat for a few minutes, a bit dazed and sad. Tears welled up, but he did not cry. Among the gifts he had been given, he realized that Angela – the one who believed in him while so many others were deriding him – had been one of the most valuable of all of life's gifts.

101

With her guidance, he had gained a sense of direction in his life, and he had had his first taste of success in moving in that direction. But he also had just lost his guide and mentor. In saying goodbye, she had expressed no regrets, only satisfaction. For Antonio, it was a confusing, bittersweet feeling.

That mood shifted, however, when he spied several butterflies skirt the wall that led into the vineyard. They were exploring. Many were taking up perches on the vines, basking in the sun. Soon, many others joined them.

Between the wall and the vineyard was a small stone shed with a weathered wooden door. From the shed emerged a man – Antonio presumed he was the children's father – who carried in his hand a sprayer. It was similar to the one that Antonio had seen wreak so much destruction back at the vineyard that had once been his. The sight of it made Antonio very uneasy.

He swooped down from the tree and began cautioning the butterflies in the vineyard to steer clear. Gina and Giorgio, still resting in the tree, strained to hear exactly what he was saying, but to no avail. Then they saw Antonio lead the butterflies from the vineyard over to a patch of ivy that clung to the wall of the house.

From there, he went about the rest of the garden, and, with an economy of words and motion, managed to convince the rest of the butterflies to assemble with the others on the ivy-covered wall.

Antonio returned to Gina and Giorgio, momentarily winded. Then he moved a few feet closer to the center of the tree, to see about Gina's condition.

"Can you still fly?" he asked.

"I think so," she said weakly. "But not for any great distance. Not just yet."

Giorgio piped up. "I can carry you, Gina. You may ride on my back – if you ever need to."

"Thanks," she said. She addressed Antonio, "But we're not going anywhere soon, *are* we?"

Antonio said, "I'm afraid so. Before the cold weather sets in. Besides, we don't belong here."

"And we belong …where?" she inquired.

"Far away, across the ocean."

"And how do you know this?"

"I had a dream."

"A dream?"

"While in my chrysalis."

"I see-e-e," she said, skeptically. "And our purpose in going there would be what?"

"To be freed from our past. To have a chance to live longer so that we actually can be of use to the next generation, so they don't grow up as orphans like we did."

"So you really believe in this dream you had?"

He paused, hearing the hinges on the back door of the house creak. The children and their grandfather were going inside. The butterfly net lay abandoned in the yard.

He turned to Giorgio. "You sure you can help Gina if she needs it? Carry her?"

Giorgio nodded emphatically.

"Let's give it a try," she said.

"All right, let's go," Antonio beckoned to the rest of the waiting butterflies.

The flight covered many miles and took several days – almost as many days as one would expect would be left in the very short life of most butterflies. They flew for hours at a time, relying on Antonio's amazing sense of direction. Through sunlight and darkness, through heavy clouds, rain and buffeting wind, the group stayed together. Periodically, Antonio would slow the pace, mindful that his followers were not in possession of his extraordinary flying skills. Despite her injury, Gina was still gamely flying on her own for the most part, occasionally piggy-backing on Giorgio.

The group crossed the northwestern region of Italy and passed through Switzerland and France. Then they crossed the English Channel during a dark, moonless night. The channel was cloaked in a dense fog, yet Antonio had no doubt he was on the right course heading toward what was to be their new home.

At dawn, to the group's relief, the fog began to break up, bringing the coast into view. They had finally reached land, flying over palisades that soared far above the English shore.

The sojourners descended into a bustling village on England's western shore, not far from the country's southernmost peninsula. Signs along the dock indicated the name of the village: Plymouth. Antonio recognized it was the same name that had come to him several times during his dreamlike state in the chrysalis. *Is this the place?* He asked himself. Other than the name, though, nothing about it seemed familiar from his dreams.

The butterflies, weary and hungry, were relieved to have some respite from their travels. Several approached Antonio and asked if this was to be their new home. Antonio shrugged. "I don't know."

Gina overheard his response. "What do you mean, you don't know? I thought you were so sure."

"Perhaps this is the place," he replied. "We'll know in due time."

Gina gestured to the rest of the group, merrily flitting about the garden. "This looks like a good place to be. To them. And to me, too." She turned to Giorgio. "How about you?"

"I leave it to Antonio," Giorgio replied.

Gina rolled her eyes and she flew away to join the others. They were alternately resting and dining among the plentiful flowers and bushes in the garden of a large estate outside the village.

Antonio flew to a promontory high above Plymouth, resting atop an ancient tree. He surveyed the village, the port and the countryside. Nothing looked familiar. Nothing recalled his dreams. The village's name was the only thing that resonated. *How could this not be the place?*

He sat in the tree for nearly an hour, sinking into a deep gloom. *What am I to tell the others? That this was all a mistake? Or should I just pretend that this is, in fact, the place I had envisioned? How would they ever know otherwise?*

Then a distracting sight came into view. Emerging from a tall hedgerow were two men, each carrying a falcon on their leather-gloved hands and forearms. Soon the falconers were putting the birds of prey through their paces, releasing them and watching them swoop, soar and, invariably, at the falconer's whistled call, return to their masters' wrists. Antonio soon forgot his worries and became absorbed with the spectacle.

His absorption quickly turned to panic as one of the birds, with amazing speed, glided quickly toward Antonio's spot on the tree. Antonio froze. His wings were paralyzed. The bird was headed directly toward him. His magnificent, imposing claws were extending.

Only one thought flashed through Antonio's mind. *This is it!? This is how the dream ends?*

Then, at the last possible moment, the bird abruptly pulled up and settled on a branch not two feet away from Antonio.

Antonio remained still, hoping not to attract attention.

Within just a few seconds, it became clear, however, that he *had* attracted the falcon's attention. The bird pivoted about on the branch and thrust his head forward, fixing his eyes on Antonio.

Then the bird spoke.

"Do you *really* think I would want to have *you* for dinner?" said the falcon.

Antonio did not answer.

"You wouldn't even make a good appetizer, my friend," he said. "Field mice, rabbits, hedgehogs, squirrels – those are more my idea of a proper meal."

Down below, one of the falconers blew his whistle repeatedly, trying to summon the falcon. Antonio could see the man blowing on the whistle, although no sound seemed to issue from it.

The falcon gave a brief, dismissive look at the falconer and muttered, "In due time, Master. In due time."

He paused, then said, "So I saw you up here, sulking," the falcon said.

"You – you did?"

"From a mile away."

"Really?"

"Well, perhaps a quarter-mile. I decided to take myself a little break from the rigors of being a raptor and pay you a visit. So, tell me, what's your story? What is your lament?"

If he had wanted to eat me, he could have done so by now, Antonio considered. *I guess it's safe to exhale. It's probably not a good idea to try to ignore him.*

So Antonio shared with the falcon his concern that he had lost his way en route to his dream. He told him about the significance of Plymouth, a place that had revealed itself as an important milestone, if not the ultimate destination, in his dreams.

"Plymouth, you say?"

"And I gather you fancy yourself quite a navigator, huh? Leading all your followers to the Promised Land?"

"I know I have a talent for navigation. It's a gift. I am certain of that."

"Well, I have another gift for you, my man. Some useful information. That being perhaps Plymouth *is* important to your plans," said the falcon.

"It is?"

"But not *this* Plymouth."

And with that, the bird recounted that he and his master, a surveyor by trade, had taken a lengthy ocean voyage to a place called New England. There the man had assisted the colonial governor in establishing jurisdictional boundaries and settling disputes about collectively- and individually- owned parcels of lands. In their leisure time, the falconer and the governor would tromp about the fields outside the village and free the falcon to hunt for, kill and retrieve rabbits and other creatures suitable for the stew pot.

"This little village – I'd guess a good two thousand miles to the west, across a vast ocean – it, too, is called Plymouth," the falcon said. "Named for the village that lies in the plain below us. The *new* Plymouth – perhaps *that* is your dream."

Again the falconer's whistle, silent to Antonio, called out for the falcon.

"I suppose I must be off," said the falcon with a sigh.

"But wait," said Antonio. "How does one get there, to New England?"

"It's simple. Heed your compass." the falcon said, chuckling.

"Compass? I have no compass."

"The one that's inside you. The gift you've been given. You're a navigator, you said so yourself, or you wouldn't have gotten this far, safely. You only fail when you fail to trust your gift and put it to use."

"Well, so far, something inside me, something I can't really explain, has caused me to lead my followers in the direction of the setting sun…"

"Apparently so," said the falcon. "You know, sometimes you'll find that true north actually isn't always north. But if it's *yours*, its direction is always true." Then he dipped, slid off the tree limb and beat his wings with enough force that the back draft nearly knocked Antonio from his perch.

Buoyed and confident, Antonio quickly departed to rejoin his followers and shared his new information about the "other Plymouth" and his conviction that they must head farther west. Much, much farther west. There was some skepticism and a lot of disappointment. Few of the butterflies relished still more days of migration.

Surprising Antonio, though, was that Gina lent her support, telling the group, "In for a penny, in for a pound. We chose to follow Antonio, and follow him we should. Look, we already – for some reason – have lived longer than any of us had a right to expect. If the trip turns out badly, well, we still will have had ourselves quite an exciting journey."

They rested for several hours, then departed. Antonio led them toward the sunset, across the peninsula and high above the ocean. There, they caught favorable wind currents. Down below them, they could see an occasional ship headed in the same direction, their sails billowing in the wind. But the butterflies, transported on a magical zephyr, passed above and beyond each ship rapidly.

In time, they reached an island off the sprawling coast. They stopped for the evening to rest and restore their strength in a moor separated from the ocean by an expanse of sand dunes.

The next morning Antonio arose early while the others were still sleeping to go into the whaling village and see what he could learn about the way to Plymouth. There, outside a rooming house, he overheard a conversation between two captains in which one of them said they would be setting sail for Plymouth later that day. Antonio returned to his fellow travelers and had them follow him to the village. Antonio tracked down the captain directing his crew in preparation to set sail. Antonio led his followers to a perch atop the ship's mizzenmast.

109

"Let's relax and arrive in style," he told them. When the morning dawned, the butterflies awoke to find the ship was anchored in a broad, shallow bay, a half-mile from what Antonio instantly recognized from his dreams as Plymouth. The sight of it triggered the recollection of another scene from his dreams, one that lifted his heart because he knew he was close. Plymouth was the way station and he was nearing *the* ultimate destination.

The butterflies once again relaxed and restored themselves, this time in a field planted with corn and squash. Antonio again took leave of them and ventured into the shabby little village, its primitive structures cobbled together from ragged stones, lime, and rough-cut wood from the thinning forests nearby. Tethered to the pier were two whaling vessels, both laden with their malodorous quarry.

Thirsty, Antonio stopped to drink from the village pump. As he clung to the sweating lip of the pump spout, he felt a tug on his folded wings. He was lifted by the pinched fingers of a ruddy-skinned, graying old man who raised Antonio to a point just a few inches in front of his nose. The man examined Antonio, then lowered him into the palm of his hand. With his other hand, he cupped the top of his palm to keep Antonio partially contained. Antonio chose to remain very still.

The man continued to study him. "What a pretty one you are," he said. "I've never seen the likes of you before – not with those colors and those big wings."

And then something strange happened. The man un-cupped his hand and then, without opening his mouth, spoke directly to Antonio using only his eyes. "I am Squanto," he said. The words reverberated slightly inside Antonio's head.

"You fear me, don't you? But I can look into your soul and see that we have a lot in common. I, too, have struggled to find my place. I tried to befriend the white men on behalf of my people. Instead, twice, Englishmen have captured me and sold me into slavery. But twice have I been released so I could serve as a guide, interpreter and advisor to these people. They've enslaved me and their diseases ravaged and finally exterminated everyone in my tribe – except me. I should hate them, shouldn't I, but yet I've found my place in the world, helping *them* find their way in this world. Now I have their respect, if not their affection. If I can do all that for *them*, why wouldn't I want to help you find your way, as well? Tell me about the place you seek."

Telepathically, just as Squanto had done, Antonio described his vision of the ultimate destination – a wide, heavily forested valley sliced by a broad and powerful river bounded by tall, richly colored bluffs – a place of surpassing beauty and tranquility. As he described it, copious details of the place sprung forth, most of which he never realized he knew before.

Squanto ruminated on this for a moment, then replied. "The place you see in your heart I have seen in person, having led the white man there."

"You have?"

"Yes. Listen to me. Follow the sunset, Butterfly. It is at least nine or ten days walk from here, winding through the woods, fording streams and rivers. But if I had wings, if the path were straight and through the sky, I imagine I could be there tomorrow or the next day. Follow the sunset. It's that simple. Find your place in the world, Butterfly."

Two days later, the butterflies had at last arrived at the place that matched the vision in Antonio's mind. They settled into a vast, beautiful, wildflower-embroidered meadow on a bluff overlooking the Hudson River. Their new home was near a small frontier village far beyond the realm of the Massachusetts Bay Colony.

The butterflies rejoiced, but also knew they would probably have only a few fleeting days left, the last days of their lives. Miraculously, they had lived well beyond the life expectancy of prior generations. Somehow the journey had extended their lives, and for this they were grateful.

They were grateful, too, that there was still time enough left in their lives for the females to deposit their larvae and ensure that there would be a new generation born in this new world.

Once the eggs had been deposited, however, something strange happened. Instead of dying, the butterflies lived on.

It was quite remarkable, the butterflies all agreed, that they were still alive as the chill of fall set in. What was it about this journey, or this new land, that was keeping them alive? They were happy, but now had new concerns. What would happen when the cold, damp days of winter finally arrived? How could they live in such conditions...and why would they want to?

Antonio, aided by Giorgio and a fully-healed Gina, scouted about for a suitable location to save his cohorts from the winter's cold. Antonio settled upon a crudely constructed barn not far from the sheep meadow. The barn was home to draft horses, milk cows and a dozen or so chickens. The barn was warm and comfortable during the chilly evenings; the hayloft would be a suitable place for the butterflies to pass the winter, and the oat bin would keep them well-fed until spring.

112

When the first snowfall hit, the butterflies were safely ensconced in the barn. On days when the sun shone and it was not too cold, they explored the valley and dallied in the newfound marvels of snow and ice. No butterfly, to their knowledge, had ever seen snow before. With the coming of spring, they became a familiar sight to the pioneer families who enjoyed watching the butterflies fluttering about the farm fields and adjacent meadows.

Antonio relished the fact that life was good for the butterflies. The land was beautiful, the food plentiful and diverse. And somehow, to his amazement, life as a butterfly had become a proposition that now lasted more than a matter of days.

Theirs was a pleasant, comfortable existence now. And his friends said he had well-earned a life of rest, a retirement to the comforts of the barn and the meadow. But Antonio did not feel entirely comfortable. In his heart, he knew that his job was not done. There were thousands of other caterpillars and butterflies back in the hills of Tuscany, trying to live through the epic drought.

These butterflies, too, needed to be saved. And he knew he was meant to save them.

*   *   *

Antonio singled out Melinda for a question. "And so what does that say to you? What was it I had learned from that experience?"

She said, "You might think you have gotten to where you're supposed to be but, actually, you never really quite finish everything you're supposed to do with your life."

"Very good!" said Antonio. "Or you can look at the lesson I eventually learned this way:

113

$\mathcal{L}$esson

"When you get to where you're going, beware the trap of settling too long into a new circle of comfort. It's a place to rest and renew, not to nest. There are always new journeys waiting for you, each one taking you to a higher or different purpose."

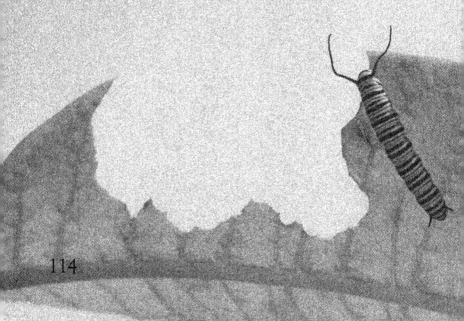

CHAPTER 11
The Accidental Embarkation

By late April, the Hudson River valley was vividly blooming, trading its decayed brown and gray winter palette for the brilliant green of nascent grasses and the regenerating foliage of trees and bushes. The butterflies dotted the landscape, their elegantly painted wings forming blossoms atop flowers and greenery of many kinds.

The butterflies were in their full springtime mode, too – just as Antonio had hoped. Larvae had been deposited in plentiful numbers around the farm and surrounding fields, and a second generation of caterpillars was just beginning to emerge.

Spring had arrived just in time. The winter had been extremely hard. The barn had provided refuge from the sometimes bitter cold, but the monotony of their confinement within the barn, and the monotony of dining on a bland diet of oats all winter long, had more than a few of the butterflies pining for "the old country."

But now those deprivations were a fleeting memory. The butterflies were intoxicated with the lengthening days, the sunshine and the kaleidoscopic world that was unfolding before them.

Antonio was well pleased with the outcome of their arduous journey to the New World. Here was a place that was a safe harbor from drought, with abundant food of immense variety. A new vineyard was in the works, and the prospect of dining on grapes from time to time brightened Antonio's spirits even more.

The night before, Antonio had shared with Gina and Giorgio his plan to return to Tuscany to lead more immigrants to this lush valley. Although he did not ask, both of them quickly offered to accompany him on the journey. He did not turn them down.

Their plan was to enjoy one more day of springtime in the valley, then retrace their flight back to Tuscany. They were intent on rescuing hundreds more butterflies from dried-up vineyards and fields and bringing them back to this lush, unspoiled new land.

On that final day, Antonio was savoring the afternoon and the spectacular views from the bluff overlooking the Hudson. He felt a small tug of regret, knowing he would miss this New World during the coming journey, and acknowledging to himself that he might not be fortunate enough to complete the trip alive.

Not far from him, near the edge of granite cliff, sat a man on a small folding stool. Before him was an easel and a canvas upon which the man was painting a landscape of the river below and the palisades across the valley.

Antonio wanted a better look, so he flew over to the painter and lit upon the man's broad-brimmed straw hat, unnoticed. As the man dabbed his paint upon the canvas, Antonio could see that a luminous interpretation of the vista was taking shape.

An unexpected blustery wind then arose, nearly causing the painting to be blown off the easel. The painter gasped as he quickly lurched forward and grabbed the wooden frame of the painting before it tore loose of the easel. The man exhaled audibly in relief, then muttered an oath, realizing that he had just smudged a portion of the painting.

On a second small folding stool next to the man was a wooden paint box, its lid propped open on its hinges. It was full of jars of paint, some open, others sealed, and a variety of brushes and several paint-smeared rags.

Antonio was fascinated not just by the painting but also by the oil paints. The spectrum of colors present, the texture of the oil and the scent given off lured him to a make a closer inspection. He dipped down into the paint box.

Not far away, perched on a budding wild rose bush, Giorgio and Gina watched Antonio and decided to join him in seeing what the painter was creating. They were making their way toward him when they were suddenly buffeted by a blast of cool wind. While struggling to right themselves, they watched, horrified, as the wind caught the lid of the paint box and carried it over the cliff, with Antonio inside.

117

Antonio was shocked as the box became airborne and plunged toward the river far below. As the box fell, the lid closed tightly and a small metal hook dropped, sealing the lid.

He was now enveloped in darkness, with paint jars and brushes tumbling all around him. One jar nearly crushed him against the bottom of the box.

At last the box slammed into the river, bottom down, and he felt the movement of the box coursing along the water, headed, he knew, to the vastness of the ocean.

* * *

Antonio paused in his story and scanned the expectant faces of the youngsters before him. Then he said, "What I found out from this misadventure about life and fate is very important for you to know and remember. The lesson learned is this:

Lesson

**"In the end, you will dis-
cover that your journey was
about returning home.** For
some that is a new home and
for others that is returning to
your original home renewed
and more passionate about life.
That home may not be as comfortable as you imagined it.
Life's lesson is not that your
'true north' is comfortable, but
that it is your path to where
you were meant to dwell."

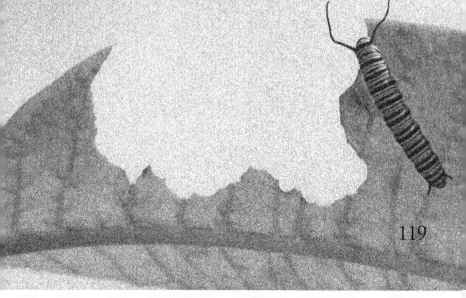

CHAPTER 12
Roaring Back

A few feet above the river, flying as fast as they could, Giorgio and Gina pursued the paint box in which Antonio was entombed. They called to him, trying to make themselves heard above the rush of the river, but to no avail.

Finally, thanks to a wide spot on the river that slowed the current, the butterflies were able to draw near the paint box. They landed on top of the box and allowed themselves to be carried along with it, bobbing and twisting in the eddies and convolutions of the current.

Calling to Antonio repeatedly, they heard no response. They inspected the latch that held the box shut. Giorgio struggled mightily to dislodge the hook, but it was no use. All they could do was stay with him, riding toward the river's end.

Inside the swirling blackness of the paint box, Antonio was struggling to maintain consciousness. It now had been many hours since he had become entrapped. The air inside was depleting. He was beginning to have difficulty breathing. Badly banged up during the box's descent to the river, Antonio heard the faint voices of Giorgio and Gina, but assumed they were nothing more than a dream.

By this time the box had been carried along for many miles. Giorgio and Gina, still sitting on the lid, saw the riverbank to their left give way to a huge expanse of green and choppy water. Then, a bit later, the river was once again confined on both sides when they reached the northern tip of an island. Along the island, thick forests alternated with meadows and low bluffs. Occasionally the pair would spot an orchard, or a field with crops or cattle.

On the river they saw more and more small sailboats and skiffs. In one case, a small cat boat nearly collided with the paint box, stirring a brief rush of fear in Giorgio and Gina.

Off in the distance they could see huge sailing vessels – some of them headed toward the island, others anchored offshore and still more tethered to the piers in the Dutch colony of New Amsterdam. Beyond they could see the smoothness of the river's current giving way to the green, sun-spangled waves of the Atlantic.

To the pair's left, on the island, they now began to pass a jumble of small, wooden frame buildings, punctuated by an occasional small farm. Then came dozens of more substantial structures hunched over the muddy lanes and cobblestone streets of New Amsterdam and the long piers of its port.

The river seemed to flow more swiftly now and Giorgio and Gina were alarmed by the prospect of the paint box being carried into the ocean. They, of course, could escape to the shore anytime they wished, but they were not going to abandon their friend. Privately, however, each of them wondered what was to become of Antonio if, in fact, he were still alive.

Then the current began pushing the box to the left, toward the island shore. The box bumped along a pebbly beach, and then caromed into some low boulders, headed under a pier and inexorably toward the ocean.

Gina and Giorgio began to despair, but then their fortunes took a sudden turn.

An old man and a young boy stood side by side along the shore, kneeling together to gut and clean several fish they had caught. They were oblivious to the approaching paint box with its butterfly passengers.

A plan was forming in Giorgio's mind. He said, "Gina, maybe they could help us."

Gina rolled her eyes, skeptical. After all, Giorgio had never been known as a thinker, much less a quick thinker.

"How so?" she said, humoring him.

He did not take the time to respond. Instead he flew from the box directly toward the boy, landing right on the lad's nose. The startled boy flailed at the butterfly, then watched as Giorgio flew back to the box.

123

"Grandfather! Look! Look!"

The old man turned and saw the box coming their way, just a few feet upstream.

"Catch it, won't you, please?" the boy implored.

The grandfather quickly rolled up his pants legs and waded out as far as he safely could, the bank dropping off precipitously only a few yards from shore. As the box floated past him, he reached out with his fishing pole and managed to arrest the progress of the box and maneuver it toward him.

He hauled in the box and gave it to the boy. The boy released the latch and opened the lid, expecting to find a treasure but disappointed only to find the paint and brushes – and Antonio's inert body. He plucked Antonio from the box, held him up and marveled at the coloring and size of the wings.

The boy tilted his head. "Is it alive?" he asked his grandfather. "Think it can still fly?"

Then he tossed Antonio into the air, to see if Antonio could fly. A slight breeze carried Antonio a few feet away, where he plopped into the river.

The shock of the cold water stirred Antonio from his unconsciousness and he began to flap his wings feebly, trying to pull loose from the current, struggling to keep his head above the waterline. His wings rapidly were absorbing water, making flying nearly impossible.

Now the water was gaining an increasingly salty taste and the waves were growing larger. The river was giving way to the ocean. Confirming this, in front of him, less than a half-mile away, he could see a clipper ship headed out toward the endless horizon of

124

the Atlantic. Unless he could get to shore soon, he knew his fate was certain – as was the fate of his mission. Doomed.

His despairing thoughts were arrested when he heard a voice calling to him. "Antonio! We're on our way!"

He managed to turn his head far enough around to see Gina and Giorgio, flying faster than they ever had before, intent on rescuing him. His heart was lifted. Then Giorgio dropped down and grasped Antonio and tried to lift him from the river. But Antonio's body had become sodden, weighted down with water. He was heavy – much too heavy. Again and again, Giorgio tried and failed to hoist his friend, with no success. Then Giorgio, exhausted, collapsed into the water himself, placing one out-stretched wing on top of Antonio's wing.

"This is it, huh?" said Giorgio, panting heavily, trying to recover.

"Maybe so," Antonio replied weakly. "Maybe so."

Several feet above them was Gina, who proceeded to scold them. "You're not giving up – you two – are you? You'd better not! We've got things to do still. There are butterflies dying back in the vineyards!"

Then she settled just above the water and grasped Antonio's flank. "I'm taking up the rear. His rear end, anyway," she called brightly, amused by her own joke. "Now, Giorgio, take a deep breath or two and take up the rest of him! Quick, before you become too soaked yourself!"

And Giorgio, casting off his despair, did as she instructed, although his wings also had become heavy from the water.

Together the two of them managed to hoist Antonio from the ocean. Flying in tandem, they headed toward a slender beach

125

along the island's shore. It was a struggle, though. They were flying into a stiff breeze, making little headway and barely staying airborne – sometimes just inches above the waves. Giorgio, already sodden from having been immersed in the water, was splashed several times by the cresting waves churning beneath him. Antonio felt Giorgio's grasp on him slipping. Gina, too, sensed Giorgio was rapidly tiring; his wings were beating much more slowly and sporadically. Antonio realized that his role and Giorgio's would need to be reversed very soon, or Giorgio would either lose his grip altogether or his weight would pull all three of them into the ocean.

Antonio began testing his strength, and his still-soaked wings. It took all the effort he could summon but he was flying. This time Giorgio clung to *him* as well as Gina.

"Hold on to us!" Antonio cried.

But Giorgio slipped a bit farther.

Antonio and Gina maneuvered awkwardly to gain hold of him. As they did so, he fell entirely from their grasp, was buffeted by the wind and carried away a few yards before he fell into the churning surf.

He disappeared below the foaming waves.

Distressed, Gina and Antonio fluttered above the water, desperately looking for him. He was nowhere in sight, so they turned their attention to the shoreline, praying that he had washed up onto the beach.

But he was not to be found.

Still, they kept their vigil – for hours. At sundown, they retreated to the top of a wild rosebush rooted in a massive dune.

There they stared vacantly toward the Atlantic, exchanging very few words, until at last a starless, moonless night removed the last of their faint hopes for their friend's salvation.

The next morning was chilly and damp, causing Gina to awaken well before dawn. Anxious, deeply depressed and longing for company, she was tempted to rouse Antonio but then reconsidered. She would let him sleep.

And so she waited. And waited. Until it was long past sunrise.

Still, Antonio remained inert, so much so that she was compelled to draw near to him and make sure he was still alive. With an outstretched wing, she tapped him several times on the top of his head. At last he awoke, casting a malevolent eye toward the steel-gray sky, and then toward her.

"What?" he grunted.

"Shouldn't we be going?"

"Where?"

"What do you mean, 'where'?" she replied. "Across the ocean, to the vineyards. The drought. To starving caterpillars dying on the vine."

"*Perhaps* there's still a drought. *Perhaps* they're still dying."

"Not perhaps. Probably!" she said.

"And as to dying, Gina, that seems to happen to those who believe in me."

"That's ridiculous."

"Oh, really? How about Aldo? Giorgio? Two close friends gone. You'd do well to stay clear of me."

127

"So you're not continuing on?"

"No. Nor returning to the valley. This is as good a place as any."

"For what?"

"To live out my days."

"Stop feeling sorry for yourself," she said. "And stop blaming yourself. Look at what you have accomplished. All those butterflies you brought to valley. Their new life. Their long life. Thanks to your leadership and navigation skills, there are many of us who have been delivered from the drought and the farmer's poison."

"As a navigator, and as a leader I am a fraud. I'm simply good at asking people for directions, for guidance."

"Everyone needs friends and allies."

"Face it. I had one great adventure. One lucky success. I will not press my luck. Or yours. Go back to the valley, Gina."

"I will not."

"I don't care where you go then," he snarled. "Just leave me alone!"

She retorted, "Fine. I will. But I'm not going back to the valley. I'm going to the vineyards. If you won't go, so be it. But I know what I am meant for – what I was put here for. Too bad you've turned your back on that."

"You're going solo?" he asked, incredulous.

"If I must."

He paused. *Another one who will fall victim to my cockeyed dreams.*

Then he said, "Suit yourself."

"So this is it? You're not going?"

128

"No."

"Then I guess it's up to me."

And with that she departed the bush, rose a few feet in the air and scanned the ocean. An eastbound vessel was only a mile or so away, a perfect opportunity to hitch a ride in the direction of the Old country. Antonio watched as she flew away. His heart grew even heavier. He sighed deeply. Then he turned his back away from the ocean and willed himself back to sleep, albeit a fitful sleep. It was beset by disturbing dreams, nightmares, really – fragments of unsettling images pulsating within his mind: Aldo being crushed under the wagon wheel; caterpillars mocking Antonio as he returned; dejected and defeated, to the vine; the vineyard scattered with the shriveled corpses of hundreds of caterpillars; the narrow escape from the wine press; the captive lion; the escape from the old man's butterfly net. And there were the images of Giorgio's demise.

Antonio awoke; his heart was pounding. He had not moved one inch from his perch since Gina had departed.

For two more nights he remained inert, occasionally nibbling on a leaf for sustenance. On the next night he could not sleep at all. A chalky gray fog enveloped the ocean and the shore. He could see nothing at all for the longest time. Then he saw a small mote of light moving in his direction, glowing and fading. It came to a hovering resting point, right in front of his face. Antonio felt some trepidation but resisted the temptation to flee.

Then came the voice. The familiar voice. "Antonio. Hello."

"Angela?" he asked. He could see no form, only light, throbbing gently.

"Yes. It's me."

129

"I can't see you."

She said, "These days there is nothing to see. No body. Only the light. The light has not died."

"But – but I thought I'd seen the last of you," he said. "You told me your work was through."

"I thought it was, Antonio. I truly thought it was. But as it turns out there is one more thing left for me to do."

"One more thing?"

"One more thing I was meant to do. You see, when there is no longer one thing you are meant to do, then the light dies. Forever."

"I don't understand.'

"Find the light, Antonio. Look inside yourself. You'll find it there. Aldo, Giorgio, Gina and all those who followed you across the ocean and to the valley, they were attracted to your light. They trusted in it. In you. The least you can do is trust in yourself."

Then her light began to retreat into the evening sky. As it did, the fog lifted.

"Goodbye, Antonio."

He followed the northward arc of the light until it disappeared into the brilliant glow of a very large and prominent northern star. He gazed at the star and pondered Angela's words, absorbing their meaning.

After a few minutes, something odd began to happen. He felt a quickening of his pulse, a liberating energy that he had not felt in a long time. And then something else happened. He was overcome by the roar of the ocean waves crashing ashore – so much louder than he had ever heard them, almost deafening. He scanned the ocean, expecting to see huge, white-capped waves beneath him. Instead the water was serene and still, reflecting the image of the full moon suspended in the eastern sky.

Passing before the moon were some wispy clouds. One of them formed the shape of a lion with a prominent mane. As the cloud floated by, the head morphed as if turning to look back at Antonio. And then the roar of the ocean was transformed into the roar of a lion.

Antonio was stirred by this sign – and he became resolute. He began to fly, setting a course in the direction of the moon. And as he did so, the roar subsided as a noise, yet its energy remained within him.

Flying higher and faster than ever before, he caught up to Gina on her way back to the Old Country. He found her perched on the crow's nest of the ship, still weeks away from the Old Country.

* * *

Melanie piped up. "And so did you make it back to the Old Country?"

A chorus of the others appealed him for the same answer.

Antonio said, "You're getting ahead of me. First the lesson learned, and that is this:

131

Lesson

"*Passion doesn't sit still.* **A life of passion is a life of moving ahead.** *If you resign yourself to live in the past or resign yourself to live only in the present with no future, you will find few sustaining rewards and very little meaningful passion.*"

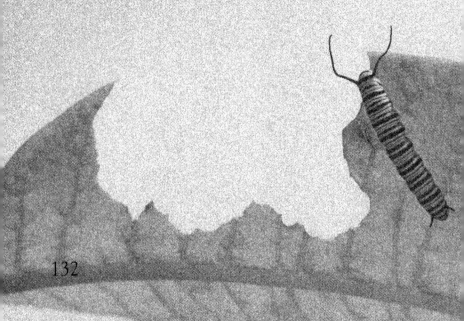

CHAPTER 13
The Way Back, the Way West

The cocooning season was drawing close when Antonio and Gina arrived. In their home vineyard and the surrounding vineyards, everywhere the depressing spectacle was the same.

Throughout the fields of Tuscany, the drought and exceptionally hot weather had continued unabated. Searing sun dominated almost every day, relieved only by occasional brief downpours that stirred hope yet barely penetrated the almost rock-hard soil. What little moisture was received often was erased by the hot breath of the dusty, late afternoon wind.

The farmers and vineyard growers throughout the region were beyond despair. Crop growth was stunted; fruits and vegetables were pathetically small. Many vineyard growers had simply given up. The grapevines were withering, stressed and diseased, as were so many of the caterpillars who feebly struggled upon the vines, seeking sustenance. What little was left on the vines to eat was the prize that precipitated many nasty skirmishes.

More than ever, the caterpillars welcomed their retreat into their cocoons. On the eve of their metamorphoses, many of the caterpillars destined to become butterflies were visited by the two weary but wise returning butterflies. They offered words of advice, encouraging the caterpillars to use their cocooning period wisely. They tried to persuade them to not just merely pass the time in the chrysalis with idle daydreaming, or backward-looking ruminations, or focusing on past failures, but instead to free their minds of mundane thoughts and open themselves instead to discovering their passions and their place in the world.

For some, this message was difficult to embrace. They had never had great expectations beyond knowing that they would enjoy a brief time as creatures with the ability to fly. Many others, though, were inspired by the words of the two disciples, and promised to themselves they would not squander their time in the chrysalis.

Gina and Antonio did not confine their work to their home vineyard. They traveled throughout the vineyards in the region, speaking to small clusters of caterpillars and attracting the interest of other butterflies and the occasional curious grape berry moth.

Thousands of miles to the west, in a meadow overlooking the Hudson, the first generations of butterfly immigrants were living a life they had not imagined possible. While the journey to the new land had been daunting, as had the prospect of living through winter confined within a barn, the rewards were many.

It was a wonderful world, this New World, the first generation agreed. They had lived longer than any butterfly had a right to expect, not just for a handful of days but now for nearly a year. They were living in a surpassingly gorgeous place that had plentiful rainfall and abundant sources of food. And since they were living so long, they actually were able to see their own offspring transformed into butterflies themselves, a grand and rewarding experience.

They loved having a connection to the next generation, although they often were dismayed at the younger generation's lack of appreciation for the treasures they so freely enjoyed, an extraordinarily long life being chief among them. Soon there would be a third generation of immigrants and (miracle of miracles) many of the first generation would survive to see them born.

The butterflies were not immortal, of course. Some of them fell prey to birds; others succumbed to illness or injury. But most of them began to realize they just might live to see another spring.

They realized they owed this bounty to Antonio, who had caused them to see that there was a better life for them away from Tuscany and that if they believed in themselves they could fly seemingly impossible distances to get there.

Now, with fall approaching there was increasing talk among the butterfly community that Antonio, Gina and Giorgio were much overdue; they might never return from their journey back to the Old Country. Antonio had told them before he left that he thought that he, Gina and Giorgio would return by the end of summer. Summer had passed many days ago, culminating in a

135

horrific hurricane, the first any of them had ever seen. It had even torn the roof off the barn.

On a crisp, windy day, a clutch of butterflies was gathered on a bush, engaged in speculation as to the fate of the three adventurers. Many of the caterpillars and butterflies surmised that the threesome had been victims of the storm as it raged above the Atlantic. As they sat there, periodically a gust of wind would separate the brilliantly colored leaves from the surrounding trees. The leaves would brush by the butterflies or occasionally cascade right onto them.

Then came a sustained wind. Was this the forerunner of another hurricane? The butterflies looked skyward, fearfully watching as trees trembled and gales of leaves streamed across the sky. One of the group remarked on what appeared to be a distant, dense flurry of leaves, very high above the ground. Another commented that the leaves appeared to be in the form of a triangle, its apex pointed in their direction. They watched, transfixed, as the wedge-shaped form grew nearer.

It then became apparent that these were not leaves at all, they were butterflies! Thousands of them.

Minutes later, as the wind died down, all of the butterfly travelers passed directly overhead, with Antonio leading the way, flanked by Gina. They glided into a sprawling meadow, their number so great that it scared a small herd of deer, browsing there for food, back into the trees, their white tails flashing.

Soon hundreds of the older butterflies hurried excitedly to the field to greet the newcomers, and to welcome the return of Antonio and Gina. Their high spirits were dampened by the sad news about Giorgio but still a celebratory mood prevailed throughout the afternoon.

As sundown grew near, a weary but content Antonio sat perched on the top of the barn where the roof had been. He watched with pride the huge cohort of butterflies fluttering about the field. They comprised, in essence, a new nation, he thought, one founded on the strength of those willing to take risks to pursue their dreams.

Still, with the new arrivals and the offspring of the first generation, there now were so many of them gathered here, he knew they would not be able to make it through another winter. The barn would not shelter them and the fields were barren.

Down in the barnyard below, the farmer and two of his sons were seated on barrels, smoking their pipes. Antonio eavesdropped as they discussed what they had heard about the abundant land and fertile soil to be found far beyond the Catskill Mountains, alongside a lake as vast as an ocean.

Antonio turned his face to watch the crimson sun drop slowly below the horizon. And as the hours passed and the moonless sky turned into an inky void, he closed his eyes and willed himself into a quiet, invisible cocoon illuminated by images of sunsets.

And in his dreams he flew toward the setting sun, no longer a butterfly but instead a winged lion – roaring for joy.

*   *   *

"And that's the story children. And it's how you came to be living here in this mountain meadow, so far away from where we first settled in this new land – and so very far away from the Old Country."

The caterpillars spoke as one, "And the lesson learned?"

"The lesson learned is this:

137

Lesson

**"All of life is about your con-
tribution. Don't die knowing that you had a gift that
you wasted.** Don't ever give
up your search for your 'true
north'. Follow the compass
that lies within you to your
personal land of dreams and
adventure."

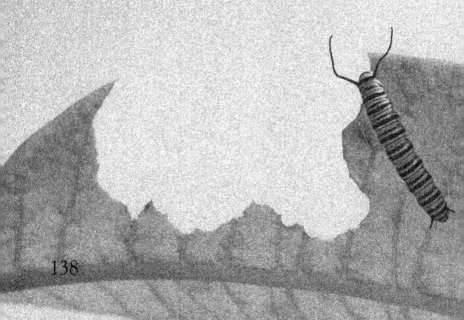

EPILOGUE

Typically, an epilogue provides a glimpse beyond the book's final chapter – a look at how the events that transpired in the book set in motion a different future for the main characters and the set of circumstances around which the story revolved.

We chose to pursue a different tack and to reflect on how the writing of the book impacted its co-author, Joseph Sturniolo, the founder of ROAR. It is his set of "lessons learned" at the end of each chapter that comprises the precepts that shape his ROAR retirement revolution workshops.

Joe's concept for the story of Antonio was that it would depict the classic hero's journey, the central construct of Joe's ROAR retirement revolution workshops.

Thus we have Antonio, comfortable in his elevated status in the ordinary world, and reluctant to move beyond his fears to pursue a more meaningful life. Then, with the encouragement of a friend, he summons the nerve to make the break, only to be dealt a damaging, humiliating blow. He retreats back to his comfort zone.

Finally new circumstances compel him to make another effort to take the leap (literally and figuratively) and break through his barrier of fear.

The journey is difficult, fraught with fears and temporary set-backs, and the definition of his destination – the realization of his gifts, of his life's purpose – is slow in coming. Immersing in purposeful self-reflection, that definition crystallizes. A series of crises test not only his abilities but also his resolve.

In the end, the journey leads to home, not in the conventional sense, but to a place he had never been before.

But of all the steps in the hero's journey, it is the *first* one – finding the courage to leave the comfort zone, to take the first tentative step – that is the hardest to accomplish.

The book made Joe think about, and more deeply appreciate, the real-life courage of some of his ROAR workshop participants who found the nerve to take the first step.

They are real heroes in their own life stories.

There is a woman we will call "Ann" who is a prime example of one of those people.

Like Antonio, Ann was deeply ensconced in her comfort zone. Like Antonio, she was a "Higher-Up," with a lot to lose by taking the leap.

When Joe first met Ann, she was the epitome of a successful baby boomer. She was a long-term career senior manager for a Fortune 100 company. She was very well-paid, not only in terms of salary and benefits, but also in "psychic income," the esteem in which she was held by others. But with decades of time with the company behind her, she was in a position to take an early retirement. She was ready for a change yet feared what leaving her job might mean for her own feelings of significance, not to mention self-esteem.

Still, something, once there, now was missing – the purpose and significance we all seem to innately long for. With encouragement from ROAR, she took a leave of absence. It was a chance to *purposefully* "cocoon" – just as Antonio did – and, as she says, "create a new blueprint for the rest of my life...and make it happen..."

She took the first step, accepting the early retirement, resolving to explore her options, knowing she otherwise never would if she were to remain in her comfort zone, distracting herself with the exigencies of her pressure-packed job.

Her resolve after taking that first step, however, was tested. She almost immediately received unsolicited, attractive job offers from companies in related fields. She could turn back on her journey and retreat to a new yet familiar kind of comfort zone.

But she stood firm, turning down those offers, realizing a mere change of corporate scenery was not the answer. Instead, she decided to enter what Joe in his workshops terms "the dark forest of wonder," searching out her options.

At this writing, Ann is coming closer to finalizing her blueprint and building her new dream.

But it wouldn't have happened without the courage to take that first step.

Almost everyone who enters the ROAR workshops and community harbors the same first-step fears.

As in the book, courage is a theme that runs throughout the ROAR workshops. Finding it. Employing it.

But there is another theme in the book that deals with courage. *Encouragement.*

The dictionary definition of encourage is "to give courage to; to give confidence to."

Too often we think of heroes as the self-sufficient type, able to tap into a deep reservoir of courage on a moment's notice and overcome their fears with no need for encouragement.

But nothing could be further from the truth.

A key precept of ROAR is that you cannot make the journey alone, you need friends, allies and mentors. Don't turn your back on them. Seek them out – not just for advice but for encouragement, the kind that will awaken the lion within you.

Antonio's friends, Giorgio and, particularly, Gina, helped provide the encouragement Antonio needed to take the first step and lead them on their journey. They continued to encourage him throughout all the tribulations of the journey.

Angela provided the mentorship.

As for allies, the two children from the market proved to be allies (as well as benign butterfly-chasing adversaries).

A ROAR participant we will call Mary acknowledges the importance of encouragement she received through the workshops: "ROAR has given me the opportunity to validate a dream I've harbored for years. I've always wanted to create a space for battered women that feels safe and secure and allows them to get back on their feet. Through the community of ROAR, I've received encouragement and validation of this dream." At this writing, she is working on the details to get the project started.

And as for needing friends to encourage her in her journey, she found one very close to home. Her husband.

"One of the most unexpected and wonderful things that has come from attending ROAR with my husband is that I never knew he had dreams before. He was guarded and quiet about them in the past. Through our ROAR experience, I have learned so much about his heart, and now we are working as a team to move toward our dreams together."

"You say you want a revolution…"
The origins of ROAR

The parable of Antonio and the "lessons learned" that conclude each chapter embody a new approach to helping people make the transition to a more meaningful, fulfilled life. The approach is aimed at baby boomers nearing retirement and others who, like the songstress Peggy Lee, ask themselves the question, "Is this all there is?" And for each of us, there is an answer, long buried in the soul's humus heap of discarded or long-postponed dreams. By taking the lessons to heart, ultimately the answer comes, not with a whisper but with a roar.

In early 2004, in a missive to his retirement planning clients – most of whom are boomers – co-author Joe Sturniolo wrote of what he termed "the anti-retirement revolution."

> *My vision for the future comes from the hundreds of people whom I have helped plan for their "retirement" over the years. Their concerns, ultimately, weren't about whether or not they had enough money to retire. They were all concerned about one big thing: "staying busy."*

143

Unfortunately, most of my clients had not been thinking about the wisdom they had now achieved, and how they might best use it for others. Now as our generation is ever-more comprised of baby boomers, how the boomers create what could be the most important time of their lives has the potential to change the meaning of retirement forever.

I have found that the passion of life lies in my battle to create the preferred future. It is a battle between what could be and what is. It is a war with our current reality and our future vision. Many of us tasted some of the passion of the battle in adolescence, but succumbed to the current reality like a frog succumbs to the boiling water because he didn't feel the pain until it was too late. I believe from my own experience and that of so many of my clients that we took the path of least resistance because we were charmed into slowly accepting each element of our current reality. We set aside the demands of our souls to instead perform the duties and responsibilities and obligations to all those we were serving.

I know I have had an itch to do something far more meaningful than helping people pick the best investments or helping them define a questionable retirement.

Those that I am helping are for the most part baby boomers. The baby boomers have always been a group who stood for something. They are hungry to find something that will use their gifts and experience and wisdom in a significant way. Some would call it a longing or hunger. Some would say we are looking for home. Some would say we are searching for self. I like to think we are searching for our place.

This was more than an essay. It was a manifesto, a statement of the challenge and the promise to create a movement – a movement that ultimately would come to be called ROAR.

While ROAR first manifested itself in workshops for his clients that later were offered to the public, in the back of his mind Joe was interested in creating a ROAR *community*, filled with people possibly just like you – looking for a change in their life, daring to put into action what they had always dreamed of doing.

Today, ROAR has succeeded in becoming a membership community promoting self-help combined with the outside help of peer mentors and professionals.

Initially seeded by the bonds created among workshop participants, the ROAR Web site (www.ROARawakening.com) has become the linchpin of the community, affording an opportunity for like-minded people to come together to chat with Joe and other members, offer tips on success or voice their fears – or offer someone a helping hand in carrying out his or her own, personal "retirement revolution."

The Workshops: ROAR workshops have been developed over the last decade by Joe Sturniolo, in collaboration with two clinical psychologists. ROAR workshops are set in three Acts, one for each of the three-day seminars: Finding the Lion Within, Arousing the Lion Within and Unleashing the Lion Within. Through an interactive process, participants are able to discover or rediscover their own unique "lion within." The passion thus unleashed has the power to propel them on a journey to a more joyful, fulfilling and meaningful life. The experience provoked in these workshops is unlike anything else available today. For example, in Act I participants take part in an imaginatively staged "safari" of hands-on experiences rather than tedious lectures. Along the way, they find their own, unique lion – the lion within *them*.

ROAR Success Stories: ROAR workshop attendees, many of them baby boomers dissatisfied or uneasy with the prospect of a conventional retirement, have been able to discover new purpose and ways to employ their long-dormant gifts for the benefit of others.

When and Where: The workshops are held at a variety of venues in ROAR's home state of Colorado and elsewhere throughout North America. For dates and times, refer to the ROAR Web site, **www.ROARawakening.com.**

"Hell No, We Won't Go!"

In the Sixties it was war –
Today it is retirement!

Co-authors Joe and Dan
expose the myth of retirement
and help you discover the 13 steps to renewal.

Find out how: **www.ROARawakening.com**

- Listen to Joe and Dan talk about the formation of ROAR and *The Caterpillar That Roared*, and share their own personal journeys.

- Listen as Joe and Dan reflect on the lessons expressed after each chapter of *The Caterpillar That Roared*.

- Listen as Joe and Dan reveal some of the secrets to "Awakening Your Lion Within".

ROAR®
AWAKENING THE LION WITHIN™

| LECTURES | WORKSHOPS |

❖ Joe Sturniolo speaks to conventions and organizations all over the world. For further information on these programs you may reach us at:

ROAR
7535 East Hampden Avenue
Suite 501
Denver, Colorado 80231 USA
Telephone (303)597-0152

❖ Corporations interested in retaining Joe for training on issues surrounding current retirement challenges please use the above information to contact us.

❖ For information about ROAR workshops visit us at www.ROARawakening.com.